Resis

— *from* —

BLACK HISTORY

for Kids

Inspiring People and Events
That Every Kid Should Know

Rann Miller

To RJ: May the Father allow you access to enjoy these stories in Glory.

To Jaxson, Kennidi, and Lyndyn: *This book was written for you, so you continue to discover the missing pages of world history and share them with your children.*

To Dad: *I'll miss you. Until we meet again.*

Text copyright © 2023 Rann Miller. Design and concept copyright © 2023 Ulysses Press and its licensors. All rights reserved. Any unauthorized duplication in whole or in part or dissemination of this edition by any means (including but not limited to photocopying, electronic devices, digital versions, and the internet) will be prosecuted to the fullest extent of the law.

Published by:
ULYSSES PRESS
PO Box 3440
Berkeley, CA 94703
www.ulyssespress.com

ISBN: 978-1-64604-445-0
Library of Congress Control Number: 2022944085

Printed in the United States
10 9 8 7 6 5 4 3 2 1

Acquisitions editor: Kierra Sondereker
Managing editor: Claire Chun
Developmental editor: Lauren Schiffman
Editor: Michele Anderson
Proofreader: Renee Rutledge
Editorial assistant: Yesenia Garcia-Lopez
Front cover design: Monique Sterling
Artwork: shutterstock.com—Nzingha of Matamba © German Vizulis; Nelson Mandela © Prachaya Roekdeethaweesab; Rosa Parks © catwalker; Toussaint L'Ouverture © Morphart Creation; Frederick Douglass © Everett Collection; raised fist © AVA Bitter; background patterns © Tania Apet
Layout: Winnie Liu

Note: Although the author and publisher have made every effort to ensure that the information in this book was correct at press time, the author and publisher do not assume and hereby disclaim any liability to any party for any loss, damage, or disruption caused by errors or omissions, whether such errors or omissions result from negligence, accident, or any other cause.

CONTENTS

FOREWORD

When people look in a mirror, they hope to see their own image reflected back to them. Somewhere in that mirror they want to see themselves. But imagine what it is like to look in a mirror and see everyone else *except* you. Or imagine what it would be like to see an image of yourself in the mirror, but it is a caricature. Being rendered something that is less of yourself has happened to Black people for hundreds of years.

For far too long, Black people were either left out of or erased from textbooks and classrooms. If we, Black people, are included, it is an inclusion wrapped in lies, evasions, half-truths, and distortions. Think of mirrors at a carnival that make a person look tall and stretched thin, or fat, or twisted, or squiggled (something that squirms or wriggles, or has loops and curls, or is S shaped or zigzagged).

In this book, Rann Miller seeks to restore Black people to the textbooks and correct the lies that have endured for centuries. As Miller makes clear, the history of Black people, even the Black people in the United States, is a part of *world* history, not only U.S. history. He challenges us to understand history through a much larger frame, a frame larger than, for example, tobacco, sugar, or cotton plantations. Miller challenges us to see history through a lens larger than a ghetto or a prison. The history of Black people did not begin with slavery or the triangular Atlantic slave system.

Black people, as a part of world history, have a history that goes back thousands of years in Africa. That history encompasses Nile Valley civilizations, ancient Nok (in what is now northern Nigeria), and numerous other ancient and medieval civilizations. (The word "medieval" refers to the European Middle Ages, roughly 500–1499 CE.) One of the great examples of medieval civilization in Africa was the Mali empire and its fantastically rich ruler Mansa Musa, about whom Miller writes.

Furthermore, people want and need heroes. For too long, Black people were left out of official history or presented only as slaves and descendants of slaves. This had several damaging effects. Not only did it whitewash history and render Black people invisible—it also taught Black people to bow down and worship white people as the only people who contributed anything of worth to "civilization" (so often defined as Europe and the West, with an obligatory mention of ancient Mesopotamia thrown in).

The omission of Black people from history also leaves Black people without heroes to admire and respect and desire to emulate. Miller restores Black heroes for the reader. These heroes range from leaders of the Haitian Revolution to Harriet Tubman, Malcolm X, Nelson Mandela, and Fannie Lou Hamer. Heroes teach us that things can be changed for the better. We are not doomed, hopeless victims. We can overcome and prevail and succeed.

Sometimes heroes are ordinary people who do extraordinary things. In 2020, a white police officer knelt on the neck of a Black man, George Floyd, in Minneapolis, Minnesota, for more than nine minutes. Floyd died as a result. This murder was filmed on a cell phone by a Black teenager, Darnella Frazier. Despite challenges and intimidation, she unflinchingly filmed the entire episode. The whole world saw the horror of what had taken place.

Darnella Frazier, an ordinary teenager, a youngster, remained determined and did an extraordinary thing. Darnella Frazier is an example of a modern hero, an ordinary person doing an exceptional thing.

Rann Miller's book is an important corrective to the omissions and distortions of past scholarship. It is a work of restoration that is long overdue. Young people and parents alike will be grateful for this valuable resource. It follows in the tradition of John Henrik Clarke, Arturo Schomburg, and Carter G. Woodson, among others, who have endeavored to teach us that Black history is a part of world history also.

Dr. Wayne Glasker
Professor Emeritus, History
Rutgers, the State University of New Jersey

INTRODUCTION

In high school, I took an honors history class during my sophomore year. The course was "World and European History." I took the course because of my love of history. I learned about the cultural, political, and economic roots of the Western world, namely, the United States, through studying the empires of Europe and the history of the Catholic Church. It was interesting. More interesting to me, though, was the question of why the school didn't offer a class on African history. The more European history I learned, the more my mind raced back to the question—where was the course on African studies?

It became clear to me that those in charge of creating classes didn't believe that Africa had a history worth exploration or study. I knew that wasn't true. Years later, I was introduced to the historian John Henrik Clarke and his writings on African history. Clarke shared in his writings that he was influenced to learn and teach the history of Africa by the historian Arturo Schomburg, who described himself as a Puerto Rican of African descent. In his first conversation with Schomburg, Clarke told Schomburg of his desire to know the entire history of African people in the world. Schomburg responded:

> What you are calling African history and Negro [Black] history is nothing but the missing pages of the world history. You will have to understand more about world history in order to understand who displaced our people from its pages.... Go study the history of your oppressor. Once you know the history of your oppressor and why he had to oppress you, you will also learn why he had to remove you from the respectful commentary of human history.[1]

That course in high school reaffirmed what all my other history courses had shown: Black history began with the triangular slave trade, and before that there was no other history worth the time to learn about. But what that course also did was lead me to reach logical conclusions: Africans must have already existed for Europeans to know that there were people to capture. Therefore, Africans had a history before the arrival of Europeans. Also, Africa had to have value that Europe did not have—in land, resources, and people—or why would Europeans venture into Africa in the first place?

I concluded that culture, knowledge, and skills were transported on those ships to the Americas. To the contrary of what I heard growing up, Africa has played a major role in the story of European domination and uniqueness. Africans provided a blueprint for explorers to reach the new world. Stolen African gold built European empires, and stolen African people built the American empire.

Black people have remained key players in the continuing story of the United States. For example, Black artists continue to shape popular culture, and Black activists push the conscience of the country to challenge injustices found in our policies and postures against one another.

The more I explored European history, the more I began to realize why African peoples were removed, as Schomburg said, "from the respectful commentary of human history."

I suspect you've also learned about European history. You've learned about the Greeks and the Romans, as well as the empires of Europe that led to the age of exploration from the fifteenth through the eighteenth centuries. You've learned about European explorers Christopher Columbus, Vasco da Gama, and Hernán Cortés. Maybe your knowledge of European history extends to the arrival of the Pilgrims on native soil they named New England—a group of people historian Joel Augustus Rogers showed weren't the desirable and hardworking people you've been taught to believe them to be.[2] Yet all you learn about the origins of the enslaved African people in the United States is this: they were once enslaved and later freed, given rights and inclusion in the society, and accomplished many feats along the way. You often learn about the first Black person to accomplish this or to become that or to gain acceptance to that place or that organization. That's the extent to what you learn.

RESISTANCE STORIES *from* BLACK HISTORY *for* KIDS

Although the entirety of the history of African people won't be told in this book, let this be your place of entry into a world of discovery, where you begin to dig into the deeper parts of the unknown. Retelling their stories can make Black history seem repetitive and boring, but I will show you that it is no such thing. Black history is rich with empowering truths that help explain the current condition in which African people throughout the Diaspora[3] and all people throughout the world find themselves; make the connection between history and the injustices you see so you are empowered to fight those injustices.

With this book, it is my goal to provide you with what Schomburg said were the "the missing pages of the world history." As Clarke said, "If we are going to be masters of our destiny, we must be masters of the ideas that influence that destiny."

CHAPTER 1

WE'RE LOOKING AT THE WORLD UPSIDE DOWN

When I was a young student, geography was one of my favorite subjects. I was fascinated with maps and locations of places. That fascination followed me all through school. Geography is one of the reasons why I love history so much, because to understand history, you must understand geography.

A DISTORTED MAP

As I was growing up, there was something I didn't understand when learning about ancient Kemet—what you probably know as modern Egypt—which thrived from 3100 to 332 BCE.[4] There were two parts of the civilization: upper and lower Kemet.

Looking at a map, I assumed that upper Kemet was in the north and lower Kemet was in the south. However, I later learned that Cairo, the capital of Egypt, was in what was lower Kemet despite being in the northern part of the region. This oddity happened because the Nile River flows from south to north and empties into the Mediterranean Sea. The idea of a river flowing from south to north didn't line up in my mind logically. Based on the maps I saw in school and what I understood of the law of gravity, rivers should flow north to south, right? The way I understood it as a child, the way gravity worked (water flowing down) must have meant north flowing south. So, the map was right. Or was it wrong? Or was I looking at the world upside down?

What Is Kemet?

Kemet is what ancient Egyptians called their land. Kemet means "Black land," or "land of the Blacks." "Egypt" comes from the Greek word *Aigyptos*, the land of Blacks. In this book, I intentionally refer to Egypt as Kemet—to honor the people who knew their land by that name.

THE TRUE SIZE OF AFRICA

Maps found in American textbooks were always wrong, particularly about the continent of Africa. For one, maps didn't express elevation from the bottom up where one can see how water flowed. Maps were pictures where one looked down from the top. You could only see a one-dimensional aspect of elevation from that viewpoint. In addition, for many years, students throughout the U.S. used the Mercator projection map created by Gerardus Mercator, a renowned Flemish mapmaker. To aid navigation along colonial trade routes, Mercator created his map in 1569 by drawing straight lines across the oceans.[5] He made Africa and South America look smaller than Europe and North America while placing Western Europe at the center of the map. Because the Mercator projection attempts to place the actual shape of the Earth onto a cylinder and not a ball or sphere, the areas closest to the poles are "stretched," both vertically and horizontally. Africa isn't stretched because the continent spans the equator, which is in the middle of the map.[6] This is all likely due to the belief in European superiority compared to all other civilization in the world.

In reality, Africa is NOT smaller than Europe and North America and can fit those continents inside of it, as well as China and India. We not only see a distorted view of Africa on many maps, but we may also be looking at the world upside down, thinking it is right side up. There is no rhyme or reason for why Europe is at the top of the map other than Europeans, like Mercator, made maps of the world and wanted Europe and Europeans to be on top.[7]

INDIGENOUS MAPMAKING

Europeans were not the only mapmakers in the world, though, nor were they necessarily the creators of mapmaking. Various civilizations, including North African societies such as Kemet and some Islamic societies, made maps of the world.[8] Roger II, an Italian king, relied on an African-born Amazigh Muslim named Muhammad al-Idrisi to design his map in the 1100s.[9]

Who Are the Imazighen?

The Imazighen (plural for Amazigh) are the Indigenous people of northern Africa. Although the Imazighen are commonly known as Berber, that is an insulting term. Arab captors assigned that name to them based on the Greek word barbaroi, meaning "barbarians." The term "Amazigh" means "free man" and has roots in the Kemetic language. The Imazighen speak languages from the Afro-Asiatic family of languages that came out of Kemet (which include Hebrew and Arabic). Imazighen people still live in northern Africa in modern Morocco, Algeria, Tunisia, Libya, and parts of Mauritania.

A reason maps made by Indigenous African people have not received the scholarly attention they deserve is due to the transfer of European mapmaking traditions to Africa during the colonial period, in addition to the ethnocentric and pejorative view that Africans did not have the cognitive ability to make maps the same way Europeans did.[10] When Europeans first colonized Africa, they decided that they were the mapmakers and not the Africans. Europeans believed that Africans were not smart enough to make maps the same way Europeans did.[11]

Ancient Greece and Rome are central to Western civilization. However, the Kemetic civilization—originating in the areas of what are now Egypt, Sudan, and Ethiopia—heavily influenced ancient Greece and Rome.[12] As a result of racism, however, that truth is withheld to take credit away from Black people and give it all to the white Greeks and Romans. To be clear, ancient Egyptians were Black people. The Greek historian Herodotus, called the "father of history," acknowledged that the Egyptians were Black people.[13] The point of highlighting this whitewashing of history is that when people put themselves at the center of history, their perspective of the world may differ from that of other people. Therefore, it is likely that throughout the Kemetic civilization, the Kemetic people's view of their civilization was actually "right side up," where the northern tip of the continent is the current country of South Africa. Since they were among the first mapmakers, their maps may be right.

The Kemetic civilization is to African Americans what Greco-Roman civilization is to architects of Western civilization: the foundation of, and introduction to, their culture and history. This was the oldest civilization in Africa, developed six thousand years ago by Africans in the rich Nile Valley.[14] So when looking through the lens of geography and history, we must always consider the origin of the information we consume to give context to the content. The source of water flow (from south to north) has to do with the region's highest point of elevation. Yet expressing that was no concern of European mapmakers. Unfortunately, much of what we learn in school is through a Eurocentric point of view, focusing on Europe and Europeans. That's the reason for the misunderstanding about the location of upper and lower Kemet.

CHAPTER 2

THE HIDDEN AFRICAN CIVILIZATIONS

When learning about ancient civilizations as a kid, I frequently heard of those located in Europe (the Greeks and Romans), Asia (the Mesopotamians, Babylonians, and Persians), and the Americas (the Aztecs, Incas, and Mayans). I did learn about the ancient Kemetic people on the African continent. My learning, however, was influenced by the accepted idea that viewed the history of ancient Kemet as something not African,[15] and the other ancient civilizations in the history of the African continent were not mentioned.

I suspect many students learn of ancient Kemet in this way. The truth is, however, that ancient Kemet is of Africa and is African. In addition, other civilizations existed on that continent before Europeans kidnapped millions of Africans and colonized Africa. The danger of failing to mention or teach about the African roots of ancient Kemet as well as about ancient African civilizations is that that absence encourages people to think that Black history began in 1619 with the arrival of Africans to be enslaved in the European colonies of what became the United States of America. Black history, however, most certainly begins in Africa.

THE CIVILIZATIONS OF EAST AFRICA: KEMET

Ancient Kemet lasted from 3100 to 332 BCE, the dynastic period. Its predynastic period dates back to 5000 BCE. Most people know of the pyramids, mummies, and hieroglyphics (a system of writing using pictures) of ancient Kemet as the major contributions of this civilization, but it has added so much more to the modern era. While most civilizations used stone tablets for writing, the Kemetic civilization created, from the papyrus plant, the earliest form of paper. The Kemetic people also created black ink; they invented toothpaste with rock salt, dried iris flowers, and pepper all crushed and mixed together.[16]

While Western historians have attempted to separate ancient Kemet from its Africanness,[17] the ancient Greek historian Herodotus repeatedly refers to the Kemetic people as being Black-skinned people with woolly hair, saying, "They have the same tint of skin which approaches that of the Ethiopians."[18] He also referred to the southern African origins of the Kemetic people, with the Nile River as the vehicle that encouraged people to migrate from inner Africa.[19] According to almost all the ancient historians, Kemet belonged to an African race that first settled in Ethiopia on the Middle Nile.[20]

Modern historian Chancellor Williams refers to Kemet as "Ethiopia's oldest daughter" based on evidence proving the southern African origin of the early Kemetic people and their civilization.[21] This evidence included archaeological discoveries (items found by someone who studies ancient societies) made in Meroe, the capital of upper Nubia—an ancient region of East Africa. There, scholars discovered that the pyramid was a building native to Meroe and only afterward reached perfection in Kemet.[22] Without question, ancient Kemet is African in essence and origin, with roots predating the dynastic period.

Who Was Lucy?

History textbooks often omit information about ancient civilizations in Africa and related facts. Information ignored includes the fact that the oldest human ancestor is African: an *Australopithecus afarensis*—an extinct species that lived around three million years ago—a specimen nicknamed Lucy who was discovered in Hadar, Ethiopia.[23]

THE CIVILIZATIONS OF EAST AFRICA: KUSH AND AXUM

Nubia was a region in the northeastern part of Africa in what's known as modern Sudan and parts of modern Egypt. Like ancient Kemet, it was divided in two: lower Nubia (in the north) and upper Nubia (in the south). Ancient Ethiopia was known as "Nubia" and not "Ethiopia" as it is known today. (The name "Ethiopia" is associated with Upper Egypt, Nubia, Meroe, Western Sudan, the Arabian Peninsula, and even India.) Another East African civilization was the kingdom of Kush, at its height between 1550 and 1070 BCE,[24] located in upper Nubia, like portions of Kemet. The Kush capital city of Meroe was regarded by the ancients as the "cradle of the arts and sciences." Hieroglyphic writing and temples were discovered there from times before the golden age of ancient Kemet.[25]

Evidence of the oldest recognizable monarchy (government ruled by a single person) in human history, preceding the rise of the earliest Kemetic kings by several generations, has been discovered in objects from ancient Nubia.[26] A Queen Makeda, better known as the Queen of Sheba, represented Kush, and she traded culture, ideas, and love with King Solomon of ancient Israel.[27] Kush was known for its ebony wood, ivory, gold, and pottery. By the ninth and tenth centuries BCE, Kemet was taken over by ancient Kush, which provided Kemet with its last age of glory and social reform under the Kushite kings of Kemet.[28]

Long before the Kushites ruled ancient Kemet—as far back as 3300 BCE—their ancestors, the ancient Nubians, lived in the area. While we don't know what they called themselves, we suspect that the name was Ta-Seti. According to Kemetic writings, this means "Land of the Bow," referring to the weapon that apparently was characteristic of people in that part of Africa.[29] Located in the northern Tigray region of what is now modern Ethiopia was the kingdom of Aksum, or Axum. Its capital city, Aksum, was huge, with a peak population as high as 20,000.[30] This wealthy African civilization thrived for centuries, controlling a large territory and access to vast trade routes linking the Roman Empire to the Middle East and India. It was known for its detailed monuments and written script, as well as for introducing the Christian religion to the rest of sub-Saharan Africa.[31]

THE CIVILIZATIONS OF WEST AFRICA: GHANA AND MALI

Several major ancient civilizations were located in West Africa or Western Sudan. One of these known to the world outside Africa was Ghana. The kingdom of ancient Ghana originated as a small settlement and emerged as a civilization rich in gold, which attracted both the Europeans and Arabs.[32]

The empire was well-organized, with a military force of 200,000 men. It reached its height during the reign of Tenkamenin, one of its greatest kings, who came to power in 1062 CE.[33] The political progress and social well-being of its people were comparable to those of the best kingdoms and empires in Europe at this time.[34] After losing its independence, the nation rose again but never returned to its previous heights. The land was absorbed by the next great empire, Mali.

From the thirteenth to seventeenth centuries, West Africa was home to the great Mali empire established by King Sundiata Keita. This kingdom united several smaller Malinké kingdoms near the upper Niger River.[35] The Malinké are a West African people occupying parts of Guinea, Ivory Coast, Mali, Senegal, The Gambia, and Guinea-Bissau. Protected by a well-trained royal army and benefiting from being in the middle of trade routes, Mali expanded its territory, influence, and culture over four centuries.[36]

The empire may be most known for its emperor Mansa Musa. ("Mansa" is a title meaning emperor.) To the outside world of the late medieval period, he was more than an individual—he *was* Africa.[37] In his lifetime, he became the symbol of the mystery and fabulous wealth of the unknown African continent, and was the flashiest of the Black kings of the fourteenth century.[38] Under Musa, Timbuktu was one of the most famous cities in the world.

After Musa's death, the Mali empire declined in importance and was overtaken by the Songhai empire, whose greatest king was Askia the Great.[39] Askia came to power in 1493 and built Songhai into the most powerful state in Western Sudan; according to historian John Henrik Clarke, his realm was larger than Europe. Encouraging scholarship and literature, the empire invited Africans and Arabs from all over Africa to study at the University of Sankore, rebuilt by Musa, in Timbuktu.[40] After the death of Askia in 1538, the Songhai empire lost strength and eventually fell to the Moroccans in 1591.

THE RICHEST MAN IN HISTORY

When we think of the richest person in the world these days, we think of Jeff Bezos, Bill Gates, Mark Zuckerberg, or Elon Musk. What if I told you that none of these individuals is the wealthiest person in history? That title belongs to African royalty. He was Mansa Musa,[41] the most famous ruler of the Malian empire. According to the website Celebrity Net Worth, Musa had a net worth of $400 billion.

To put that in perspective, his adjusted net worth of $400 billion tops Musk's net worth of $340 billion in September 2021, John D. Rockefeller's $340 billion (who made his fortune in the oil business), and Andrew Carnegie's $310 billion (who made his fortune in the steel and railroad industries).[42] The difference between Musa and the number two placeholder, Musk, is $60 billion, which looks like $60,000,000,000. That is a lot of money.

THE LEGACY OF MUSA

When Mansa Musa rose to power in Mali, the kingdom occupied territory that made up the former empire of Ghana. Musa ruled from 1312 to 1337. He took over the kingdom of Mali from Mansa Abu Bakr. There is debate about whether Abu Bakr was Musa's father, grandfather, or uncle, but Musa took over Mali after Abu Bakr's departure in search of the New World. According to historian Ivan Van Sertima, Abu Bakr left with a company of men, supplies to consume and trade, and gold in search of new lands across the Atlantic Ocean. He left Musa in charge and never returned.

Musa was known for his wealth and his flashiness. He sat on a large ebony throne on a raised platform with elephant tusks along the sides, with an enslaved person holding a large silk sunshade topped by a figure of a golden falcon. When he met with people, he carried gold weapons, including a bow and arrows (symbols of royal power in Mali).[43] Music featuring various instruments—including different sizes of drums, trumpets made of elephant tusks, and a kind of xylophone, called the *bala*, famous for its beautiful sound—accompanied his public appearances.[44]

HOW DID HE GET SO RICH?

Ghana was known for its gold, among other resources. However, Musa expanded his empire, stretching it about two thousand miles, from the Atlantic Ocean all the way to what is now Niger. He took over parts of what are now Senegal, Mauritania, Mali, Burkina Faso, Niger, the Gambia, Guinea-Bissau, Guinea, and the Ivory Coast.[45] With greater territory came increased resources, including gold and salt; according to the British Museum, the gold the empire possessed amounted to half the world's gold at that time.[46] In his lifetime, Musa symbolized the mystery and fabulous wealth of the largely unknown African continent.[47]

Musa's Reputation

Musa's reputation was so widely known throughout the world, particularly in Europe, that the *Catalan Atlas* map featured an illustration of him at its center. Spanish mapmakers created this atlas of the medieval world around 1375; it included depictions of trade routes near and through the Sahara and was widely considered the most important map of its time. Knowledge of Musa and his riches spread when he made a pilgrimage across Africa to the Arab world.

THE PILGRIMAGE TO MECCA

Musa was a Muslim, a follower of the religion of Islam. One of the five pillars of the faith is the hajj, or pilgrimage to the Muslim holy city of Mecca (now in Saudi Arabia) to visit the Kaaba ("the cube" in Arabic). Muslims consider this to be the house of God that contains the sacred black stone. Performing hajj is something Islam calls for every Muslim to do at least once if they are physically and financially able.

Musa was both, and in 1324, he made the four-thousand-mile trip to Mecca. He didn't make the trip alone, or quietly. He went in regal splendor with an entourage of sixty thousand people. This included twelve thousand enslaved people and eight thousand companions, each carrying a staff of pure gold, who marched in front of him.[48] In addition, 280 camels bore 2,400 pounds of gold, which the emperor distributed as gifts.[49]

When Musa arrived in Egypt in July 1324, his huge caravan camped outside Cairo near the Great Pyramids. This created a great sensation because he carried such a huge amount of gold with him and was extremely generous in his gift giving.[50] In fact, so much gold flowed, according to History.com's Thaddeus Morgan, that it devalued the metal and led to a currency crisis that took Egypt twelve years to dig itself out of.[51]

Musa gave away so much of the precious metal in the Muslim holy city of Mecca that year that gold lost value in the region.[52] When Musa returned to his kingdom, he brought back an architect (a person who designs buildings) who designed impressive buildings in cities of Timbuktu, Gao, and other parts of his realm; Musa also improved education throughout the empire.[53] The kingdom of Mali reached its greatest size and influence around the same time, prospering as a bustling, wealthy kingdom, thanks to Musa's expansion and management.[54]

CHAPTER 4

A CHOSEN LAND AND A CHOSEN PEOPLE

When learning about the slave trade as a student, I often wondered: what was it about the Africans that encouraged the Europeans to capture, enslave, torture, and dehumanize them? It was a question none of my teachers could accurately answer. They often responded that European empires were more technologically advanced than other civilizations throughout the world, including African societies.

I guess the idea behind this statement was that the Europeans thought they were better than other people and it made sense to enslave others because the Europeans were more advanced. But from what I had already learned about African society during those times of enslavement, I knew that European empires weren't more advanced. Sadly, all my grade-school education had to offer was the information found in history textbooks, which revealed very little about African enslavement.

The Traditional History Textbook

The traditional history textbook too often romanticized the Dark Ages, played up the Renaissance, glorified the age of exploration, and announced the industrial revolution as the dawn of the modern age. The Dark Ages, also known as the Middle Ages, was the time in Europe between the collapse of the Roman Empire and the beginning of the Renaissance. It is considered to be a period of backwardness in all facets of life and society; as the rest of civilization progressed culturally, economically, and intellectually, Europe was declining in those areas.

THE ROOT CAUSE

Textbooks in school largely failed in teaching African history but never failed to reveal that Africans were taken from their homes to be enslaved. In their telling of European history, these textbooks failed to explain the reasoning for stealing human beings from Africa. Europe's age of exploration, from the fifteenth to the seventeenth centuries CE, and internal strife in West Africa were factors contributing to the start of the slave trade.[55] With the opening of the New World and the expulsion of the Moors—Muslims from northern Africa and the Imazighen tribes—from Spain during the latter part of the fifteenth century, Europeans started to expand beyond their homeland into the broader world.[56]

Who Are the Moors?

Textbooks are likely to mention these Arab peoples who ruled Spain for roughly seven hundred years only in terms of the conquest of the Iberian Peninsula, the location of what are now Spain and Portugal. The Moors included both Muslims from northern Africa and the Imazighen, who invaded and occupied Spain and portions of France from the eighth to the fifteenth centuries CE. Europeans created the term "Moor" to specifically describe these members of the Imazighen tribes. This military conquest was chiefly an achievement of Black Africans under the leadership of African general Gebel Tarik, also known as Tarik ibn Zeyad.[57]

The argument for the slave trade had already begun in Europe with attempts to defend the enslavement of other Europeans, who had become captives—people taken prisoner—as the result of religious wars between European nations over hundreds of years.[58] Sadly, peace was rare throughout the continent. Kings ruled with cruelty; education wasn't available to all; and farmers had no land and had to farm on the property of rich landlords who had private armies to squash any rebellion.[59]

WHAT MADE THE CONTINENT OF AFRICA THE TARGET?

Meanwhile, African kingdoms flourished in West Africa or Western Sudan. After a thousand years of glory, however, many of these West African states were suffering from internal disputes. This led to a decline and therefore weakness among those nations, making it hard for them to resist the slave trade.[60] In fact, when the Moors were expelled from Spain, they returned to Morocco, where they arranged to invade the Songhai empire, an invasion that caused many of those internal disputes.[61]

Where Is Western Sudan?

When hearing of Western Sudan, you may think of the western portion of the current nation of Sudan. But Western Sudan refers to the area of West Africa right below the Sahara Desert that was home to the empires of Songhai, Mali, and Ghana. This is home to the modern West African nations of Nigeria, Ghana, Benin, Ivory Coast, Mali, and Sierra Leone.

In addition, African societies dealt with people differently than European societies. African societies relied on the goodness of nature to provide the people with food, land, and basic necessities. Land was neither sold nor bought because the land belonged to everyone.[62] As for Europeans, their society at the time was one in which people had to compete for their breakfast, their land, and their mate; Europeans had developed a competitive nature that Africans could not deal with.[63]

DON'T BELIEVE THE HYPE

It is not that African people were inferior warriors, because history is rich with examples of African warriors who resisted European explorers. It's not that Africans weren't travelers first, because there is a rich history of Africans who traveled to Europe, Asia, and across the Atlantic prior to the age of exploration.

It is not that Europeans believed that Africans were the only people made to be enslaved, because Europeans enslaved other Europeans. Instead, the reason Europeans were able to enslave Africans is that Europeans were opportunistic, meaning that they took advantage of the tools they had to get what they wanted. They were equipped with a tool of torture: gunpowder. And they took advantage of people in countries with internal conflict while those Europeans were in search of resources, like gold, land, and people.

What is also true is that to justify the destruction of African societies by the slave trade, racism was created. It was the Western European belief system that created racist stereotypes, like Africans were "savages." Lastly, to excuse European enslavers, some will say that Africans are just as guilty for African enslavement because they actually traded away their own people. But the truth is that Africans had a different definition of enslavement than Europeans did— enslaved people (particularly Africans) weren't considered property by Africans. Europeans did consider enslaved Africans as property. (See "The Great Escape of Ona Judge" on page 42 for more on enslaved persons as property.) It's possible that if Africans knew how Europeans treated their enslaved persons, they wouldn't have agreed to take part in the trade.

CHAPTER 5

THEY CAME BEFORE COLUMBUS

For many U.S. students, the first day off during the school year is Columbus Day, honoring the explorations and "discoveries" of Christopher Columbus. A major problem with this is that the idea that Columbus discovered something ignores the existence of the Indigenous people living throughout the Americas and the Caribbean. In response to that, Indigenous Peoples' Day[64] replaces Columbus Day in seventeen states.

This day honors First Peoples rather than a colonizer associated with the massacre of First Peoples and their subsequent assimilation (the process of being made a part of the culture of others) into the culture of a colonial power. In addition, Columbus didn't discover the New World because he wasn't the first to arrive in the New World from overseas, and he knew it. Africans arrived in the New World prior to European explorers such as Columbus. The knowledge of this was a major factor that drove Columbus's desire to search for new lands.

CONFIRMATION OF THE GUINEA ROUTE

When meeting with the Portuguese king in 1493 after his first voyage to the Caribbean, Columbus figured that the king wanted to speak to him about the continent of Asia. However, the king informed Columbus of another world that was south and southeast. He said that Africans had traveled to that world, and it could be found near the equator, parallel to the land of Guinea in Africa.[65] According to the king, "Boats had been found which started out from Guinea and navigated to the west with merchandise."[66]

This was new information to Columbus, so he paid attention. The reason for the meeting was that the king desired an imaginary line to divide the New World between his nation—Portugal—and the

Spanish. He thought this would give the Portuguese the upper hand in laying claim to South America. But Columbus saw an opportunity to secure his own wealth. Eventually, the Spanish did agree to this line in the Treaty of Tordesillas, a deal brokered by Columbus. This treaty is responsible for Brazil becoming Portuguese territory and the remainder of the Caribbean and South and Central America becoming largely Spanish territory.

Columbus's plan was to take advantage of both nations to profit as much as possible from both. He did not tell the Spanish about the route to the New World from Guinea so he could claim discovery and the fame and fortune that came with it. He later withheld details about the route (after he traveled it) from the Portuguese. Rightfully, the Spanish didn't trust Columbus, but he promised there was nothing of value east of the line and that all the riches lay west. With that, the Spanish sent Columbus out to voyage on their behalf. While on his second voyage, he found what the Portuguese king told him to be true: a dark-skinned people were trading with the Indigenous people of the Caribbean islands. Columbus figured out that they were people from the coast of Guinea or West Africa.[67]

Africans Found in the Caribbean

According to Columbus's diary, "The Indians of this Espanola said there had come to Espanola a black people who have the tops of their spears made of a metal which they called gua-nin,[68] of which [I] had sent samples to the [Royals] to have them [examined], when it was found that of 32 parts, 18 were of gold, 6 of silver, and 8 of copper."[69] (Van Sertima explains the root of the word guan-nin in They Came before Columbus: "The origin of the word guanin may be tracked down in the Mande languages of West Africa, through Mandingo, Kabunga, Toronka, Kankanka, Bambara, Mande, and Vei. In Vei, we have the form of the word ka-ni which, transliterated into native phonetics, would give us gua-nin. In Columbus's journal, "gold" is given as coa-na, while gua-nin is recorded as an island where there is much gold.")

TRAVELING THE GUINEA ROUTE

African spear tips presented by the Indigenous people of the Caribbean islands helped confirm the existence of the Guinea route mentioned by the Portuguese king.[70] This gave Columbus the confirmation necessary to take that route in search of South America. But he did so under the banner of the Spanish crown and not that of the Portuguese. He did this not because he preferred the Spanish over the Portuguese but because word got to the Spanish that a land existed beyond the Caribbean, and they hired Columbus to find it and claim it for Spain. In May 1498, Columbus set off on his voyage, taking the Guinea route to South America.

The journey along that ocean route was fast and calm, but the trip was made for Africans far more than the Europeans.[71] Columbus was so scared of the sun while on the trip that he feared the ship would catch on fire. Fortunately for Columbus, the rains came, and nothing burned. By August of that year, he had settled along the South American coast, where the Indigenous people brought woven cotton handkerchiefs with patterns and colors that closely resembled those brought from Guinea.[72] These were the earliest documented traces of the African presence in the Americas. Without his knowledge of the Guinea route, who is to say that Columbus would have ever found South America?

MORE EVIDENCE OF AFRICANS IN ANCIENT AMERICA

The Mandingo people of the Mali and Songhai empires, and possibly other Africans, crossed the Atlantic to carry on trade with the Western Hemisphere Indians. They even succeeded in establishing colonies throughout the Americas.[73] Historical records list the dates of these journeys at the time that Askia the Great ruled the Songhai empire.[74] Columbus and other early Europeans returned with evidence that African peoples had already reached those shores. On his voyage to the Americas, the Italian explorer Amerigo Vespucci witnessed Black men out in the Atlantic Ocean returning to Africa.[75]

Evidence of African settlements includes early European explorers on the Isthmus of Darien (now Panama) finding skulls identified as African.[76] The largest Black colony appears to have been a permanent settlement at Darien, where the Italian explorer Vasco Núñez de Balboa saw Africans in 1513[77] and believed they had sailed from Ethiopia.[78]

In addition, a notable tale from Peruvian traditions tells of how Black men from the east had been able to penetrate the Andes Mountains.[79] Furthermore, Indigenous traditions of Mexico and Central America indicate that Africans were among the first occupants of that territory; some Indigenous people claim they descend from these same Africans.[80] Also, the language of the Indigenous people features certain words that are originally African, such as "canoe" and "tobacco."[81] Because of this evidence, it is understood with a high degree of certainty that Africans braved the roaring waters of the high seas and established relationships with the Indians of the Americas well over a thousand years ago.[82]

CHAPTER 6

THE QUEEN CALLED KING

Black History Month celebrations are great opportunities to learn about African Americans who made contributions to both the African American community and the United States as a whole. When I was in school, it was one of the only times when I would learn about Black women who led people and entire movements. Certainly, we learned about Harriet Tubman leading enslaved Black people to freedom. We also learned about Shirley Chisholm, who was the first African American woman to run for a major party's nomination for president of the United States.

But in my learning about African women beyond the realm of the New World, those lessons were nowhere to be found. It's not that the information wasn't out there, but I believe that many of my teachers were unaware of African history and the history of African women serving as leaders. One such leader served in both the government and the military: the renowned warrior queen Nzingha of Matamba.

WHO WAS QUEEN NZINGHA?

Nzingha was born a princess in 1583; she was the sister of King Ngoli Bbondi, the king of Ndongo (in what is now Angola).[83] At the time of her birth, the Portuguese were establishing themselves on the continent of Africa, specifically West Africa, in search of gold. However, Nzingha was born ready for a confrontation. She belonged to the Jagas ethnic group—an extremely militant group that formed a human shield against the Portuguese conquest of the country and was always on the military offensive.[84]

The Portuguese Arrival in Africa

Portugal wasn't the only European power active during the age of exploration and colonization. But a treaty with the Spanish allowed the Portuguese to conquer all territories east of an imaginary line. This meant that most of South America, the Caribbean, and North America were for the Spanish (the British and French entered the picture with the fall of the Spanish in the Anglo-Spanish War between 1584 and 1604). As the British, Spanish, and French conquered the New World, the Portuguese set their sights on Africa, primarily for gold from West Africa.

When Nzingha became an adult, she not only joined her army but also led a military unit of fierce women warriors, winning battle after battle.[85] In 1622, her brother asked her to negotiate a peace treaty with the Portuguese, who wanted to take over the kingdom as part of their quest for gold. But after her brother died and she became queen of both lands in 1632, she intended to resist the Portuguese and ultimately expel them. As queen of both her and her brother's kingdom, Nzingha began to strengthen her power. One way she did this was by forbidding her subjects to call her queen and ordering them to call her king.[86] Another way was by dressing in men's military clothing when leading her army into battle.[87]

Nzingha was a very intelligent ruler. In her ambition to strengthen and expand her kingdom as the Portuguese attempted to use their influence and gain power in the area, she persuaded so-called slave soldiers under the control of the Portuguese to leave the Portuguese side and fight alongside her. This resulted in thousands of slave soldiers deserting the Portuguese and joining her forces, which created a serious security problem for the Portuguese.[88] Aided by her alliance with the Dutch, Nzingha was able to resist the Portuguese and defend her people for decades, striking fear into the Portuguese with her woman warrior army.

NZINGHA'S DECLINE

The turning point in the struggle against the Portuguese came when the Portuguese kidnapped Nzingha's sister, whom she loved dearly, and beheaded her as a prisoner of war.[89] This led to Nzingha signing a treaty with the Portuguese in 1659 to keep the peace. With this and all other treaties, however, Nzingha never paid financial tribute to the Portuguese, nor did she recognize them as overlords of her and her people.[90] But at this point, she was seventy-five years old, and many of her supporters within the kingdom had either given up the fight or died.

On December 17, 1663, this great African woman died. With her death, the Portuguese occupation of the interior of southwest Africa and the massive expansion of the Portuguese slave trade began.[91] Although her death resulted in a power vacuum that the Portuguese eventually filled, her life represents the resistance and rebellion against colonization and enslavement shown by numerous African women leaders in government and military. These strong women include businesswoman Madame Tinubu of Nigeria; Nandi, mother of the great Zulu warrior Shaka; and Kaipkire, a warrior of the Herero people of southwest Africa.[92]

CHAPTER 7

THE BIRTH OF A NATION

The founding of the United States had more to do with power and control than liberty. I was taught that various British government acts (the Tea Act, Stamp Act, Townshend Act, and so on) led to the American Revolution. The truth is, what really brought about the desire to break away from Great Britain were two events that the textbooks I used omitted. These were the Molasses Act of 1733 and the British court case Somerset v. Stewart.

THE MOLASSES ACT

Molasses mattered because it was the main ingredient in rum, and molasses was traded in West Africa for African people to enslave. Although molasses wasn't the same as money, as an ingredient in rum, molasses was a highly sought-after commodity. Money made from or items traded for molasses fueled such industries as fishing, shipbuilding, cattle rearing, and, of course making alcohol, but it also helped make African enslavement possible because molasses was currency.[93] Molasses was the foundation of the slave trade and at the root of the financial growth of New England, as well as the thirteen colonies.[94]

The initial problem for the New England colonists was that England was the chief supplier of African labor by way of its rum. However, the colonists were able to acquire molasses cheaply from the Caribbean, use the molasses to make better rum than English rum, and then trade the rum for African labor. This was the new triangular trade: New England, Africa, and the Caribbean.[95] (This partially replaced the previous triangular trade between Europe, Africa, and the New World.) Angered by the colonists cutting them out of profits, the British tried to charge a tax, the Molasses Act of

1733, on all imported molasses and on purchasing British molasses. The colonists defied the tax and were able to smuggle in imported molasses until 1764. Once the British required the colonists to help pay for its wars, the Molasses Act of 1733 was revived as the Sugar Act of 1764.[96]

The Focus on the Stamp Act

Africa's Gift to America reveals, "Rum and the slave-trade are not glamorous and patriotic items therefore most... textbooks omit them. Instead, stress is laid on the Stamp Act," which called for Americans to use an official stamped paper for all legal documents. "The molasses and sugar acts had struck directly at the slave merchants.... But the Stamp Act and the tax on tea affected all, especially the masses, and were thus much more effective issues for capturing general discontent." The real issue, though, was the rivalry between the wealthy slave owners of New England and those of Great Britain.[97]

This act motivated the New Englanders to consider independence. One of the U.S. founding fathers John Adams said, "Molasses was an essential ingredient in American independence."[98] However, it would take something else for the Southern colonists to join their line of thinking.

SOMERSET V. STEWART

This event begins with a nine-year-old African child who was kidnapped, brought to Virginia, and given the name Somerset by his twenty-four-year-old captor, Charles Stewart. Stewart "trained" Somerset as his personal servant, and Somerset served in this role for the next twenty years.[99] In 1769, Stewart traveled to London, England, to help raise his sister's children after her husband died, and he took Somerset with him.

There, Somerset got to know the city and found a Black community of free and fugitive African people. Two years later, in 1771, Somerset left Stewart's home in London and never returned. Stewart hired hunters of enslaved persons who caught Somerset and held him on a boat set for Jamaica so he could be sold. But because he was baptized, Somerset had godparents, and they petitioned the court, saying that Somerset was being held against his will.

Somerset was released and required to appear in court to determine the state of his freedom. In 1772, the judge ruled that Somerset couldn't be held in bondage.[100] This decision struck fear into the hearts of the Southern colonists; they feared that if enslavement were abolished in England, abolition would come to the colonies, and enslavement had made those colonists rich.

They believed this might come to pass because of the Declaratory Act of 1766, in which the British Parliament claimed total power over "all cases whatsoever" in the colonies.[101] When northern colonial leaders, including Adams, agreed to maintain enslavement as an institution if independent from England, all colonies agreed to declare independence. And the rest, as they say, is history.

CHAPTER 8

L'OUVERTURE AND THE TAKING OF SAINT-DOMINGUE

When I started learning about enslavement as a high school student, I always wondered what would happen if all the enslaved Africans had taken over and started their own country. I asked that one day during a Black History Month lesson in Sunday school (Christian education classes before church services). To my shock, a friend of mine said that's what happened in his country. He was Haitian.

In 1630, the French came to the island of Hispaniola, now Haiti and the Dominican Republic. The Spanish occupied the eastern side of the island, and with the labor of enslaved Africans, the French took control of the western side. The French side of the island, named Saint-Domingue at the time, became the crown jewel of France[102] and the richest European colony in the Western Hemisphere.[103]

THE RACIAL MAKEUP OF THE ISLAND COLONY

The French settlers were colonizers, coming to the land and establishing political control for economic gain and political influence. The French kidnapped Africans from their homelands and took them to the island to exploit them for profit. They also exploited the Africans politically, as the enslaved Africans had no rights. In addition to the Africans and the French, biracial individuals, called mulattoes, lived on the island. A mulatto was a person of mixed ancestry; here, mulattoes were a mix of French and African ancestry.

The term originated from the Spanish word *mulato* and meant "mule," an offspring of a horse and donkey. The term is outdated and offensive. It appears here only to expose how the French referred to biracial individuals. Mulattoes were free and considered superior to enslaved Africans, but they had no real social standing because they were not white. The use of the term "white" instead of "French" is purposeful here because any European person (whether French, Spanish, British, and so on) had social standing and white privilege that nonwhite people, namely, the Indigenous and African peoples, did not have.

What Is White Privilege?

The word "privilege" refers to benefits given to a person or specific group of people. White privilege means that because people are socially categorized as white, they have advantages in society that other racial and ethnic groups lack. For example, white people can walk, shop, or drive without being harassed. But nonwhite people—particularly Black people—don't enjoy similar privileges, that is, freedom from harassment, because of racist thinking and policies.

PIERRE DOMINIC TOUSSAINT

Pierre Dominic Toussaint was born enslaved in Hispaniola in 1743. His father was a captured prince of the Arradas, a powerful tribe on the coast of West Africa, whose grandfather was king.[104] Toussaint—and his fellow enslaved Africans—experienced harsh and bitter treatment by the French. The cruelty of enslavement planted the seeds of rebellion among the African people, who found inspiration in the French Revolution of 1789.

The biracial people of Saint-Domingue, who had no role in formal government on the island, sensed an opportunity with the fall of the French monarchy (government ruled by a single person) after the French Revolution. They sent representatives to Paris, France, to petition for the right to rule on the island. The French tortured and killed those representatives to warn any other nonwhites not to attempt such a thing again. This injustice encouraged Toussaint to actively plan a revolt.[105]

TOUSSAINT BECOMES L'OUVERTURE

While the French leader Napoleon Bonaparte was busy at home fighting European powers in the Napoleonic Wars (1792–1815), Toussaint organized enslaved men in the forests of Hispaniola.[106] He pushed into the eastern part of the island, winning battle after battle. He pushed out the Spanish and then turned his attention to the French. He beat the French so badly, and so often, that his victories earned Toussaint the nickname L'Ouverture, meaning "the Opener," and the title, General of Saint-Domingue.[107]

Toussaint was a nation builder. Once he removed the Europeans by force, Toussaint became a leader and urged white, African, and biracial inhabitants to put aside their differences and unite for the good of the land. In addition, he built roads, improved agriculture, and built schools.[108] He made a new constitution and declared himself governor, angering Napoleon, who considered Toussaint "a rebellious slave."[109]

Toussaint called himself "a Black Bonaparte," a comparison that caught on among his admirers in France, as well as Napoleon's enemies in France who went further, saying that "of the two Bona-partes, the Black one is greater."[110] Thus, for Napoleon, recapturing Saint-Domingue was both a business and a personal matter. He said, "My decision to destroy the authority of the Blacks in Saint-Domingue is not so much based on considerations of commerce and money, as on the need to block forever the forward march of Blacks in the world."[111]

Who Were the Taino?

The Taino are the Indigenous people of the Caribbean islands. They lived throughout the Caribbean, but the Taino inhabiting the Greater Antilles were the Arawak people. Around 400 BCE, they gradually began developing settlements on the island of Hispaniola.[112] Although the Taino were declared extinct by 1565, their descendants still exist in Greater Antilles' nations due to intermarriage between the Taino and the Spanish.

FROM L'OUVERTURE TO DESSALINES

In 1801, Napoleon sent an army of fifty thousand soldiers to restore French rule over Saint-Domingue. Toussaint was eventually captured and exiled to France, where he died in a French prison in 1803.[113] However, all was not lost for the African people of Saint-Domingue. Jean-Jacques Dessalines, Toussaint's second in command, took over for Toussaint and outsmarted the French, who were now back in control after Toussaint's capture. Dessalines tricked the French into thinking he was on their side to prevent their murdering of the Haitian rebels—long enough for outbreaks of malaria and yellow fever to reduce the numbers among the Frenchmen whereby the Haitians could defeat who was left. From there, Dessalines and his armed forces defeated the French in 1804 and secured liberty for the people from the French.

Dessalines took the French tricolor flag and ripped the white out, leaving only the red and blue to represent African and biracial people. In honor of the Indigenous Taino inhabitants of the area, he renamed Saint-Domingue as Hayti, the Taino name for the territory before the arrival of the Spanish.[114] It means "land of high mountains" in the Taino language. To ensure peace in what is now known as Haiti, Dessalines abolished enslavement, declared that no white man would ever enter Haiti with the title of master, and declared all people of African descent—regardless of complexion—would be known as Black.[115] The people elected Dessalines as president of the newly formed nation. (See "Haiti and El Libertador's Great Betrayal" on page 47 for more on Haiti upon its liberation.)

THE MOST SUCCESSFUL REVOLT OF THE ENSLAVED AFRICANS IN HISTORY

This revolt became known as the Haitian Revolution. It is the only successful rebellion by the enslaved throughout the Western Hemisphere that resulted in the creation of a nation. Its success deeply concerned slave owners in the United States. They feared that this would encourage members of their enslaved population to rebel against their captors. This fear led to the continuous demonization and mistreatment of Haiti by the U.S. and France through imperialist actions. In exchange for freedom, France demanded reparations for losses it suffered while occupying the nation and during the Haitian Revolution as well as for future losses from the lack of slave labor.

Imperialism is a policy of exerting or extending political or economic power and influence over a territory by use of (often military) force. The imperialist actions in this case were payback for the actions of Toussaint and Dessalines. Napoleon not only abandoned his effort to recapture Saint-Domingue but also gave up the Louisiana Territory, including New Orleans, to the United States. He chose to focus on strengthening France's colonial holdings in the Lesser Antilles islands. Thomas Jefferson, the president of the United States at that time, offered the French $10 million for New Orleans in 1800; Napoleon sold the entire Louisiana Territory to the United States for $15 million in 1803.[116]

For the United States, Haiti represented inspiration to enslaved Blacks in the country to strive for their freedom. As a result, Haiti was a natural enemy; the existence of a Black power was a threat to a white settler colony.

BY THE NUMBERS: TRANSATLANTIC SLAVE TRADE*

12.5 MILLION

Africans shipped to the New World from 1525 to 1866

26%

Children on average per slave ship

15%

Africans who died during the slave trade

50.8%

Percentage of Africans taken from the continent and shipped to the Carribean from 1525 to 1866*

35.2%

Percentage of Africans taken from the continent and shipped to Brazil from 1525 to 1866*

3.6%

Percentage of Africans taken from the continent and shipped to the United States from 1525 to 1866*

35,000

Highest number of Africans brought annually to the US (between 1619 and 1865)

88%

Population of Black people enslaved in the U.S. in 1860

60%

Enslaved population located in the U.S. by 1860

*   Henry Louis Gates, "Slavery, by the Numbers," *The Root* (February 10, 2014), https://www.theroot.com/slavery-by-the-numbers-1790874492.
    Brendan Wolfe, "Slavery by the Numbers (Redux)," *Encyclopedia Virginia* (August 24, 2017), https://encyclopediavirginia.org/slavery-by-the-numbers-redux.
    "Transatlantic Slave Trade Database," SlaveVoyages, accessed November 14, 2022, https://www.slavevoyages.org/about/about#.

CHAPTER 9

THE GREAT ESCAPE OF ONA JUDGE

What you always learn about as a kid are the former presidents of the United States. While I was driving my kids to the store, my daughters were singing a song they learned in school to help them remember the names of all the presidents. You may have learned a similar song. The song, of course, paints these men in a positive light. However, history is never simple. It is complicated and filled with very complicated people. One such person is the first U.S. president, George Washington.

Washington is considered a national hero for his role during the American Revolution, but he also held human beings' captive. He was an enslaver for fifty-six years of his life, holding over three hundred African peoples and Black people of African descent captive. Upon learning this, I was introduced to the truth that had I lived during the time our country was formed, I would have been a captive of some white person.

Washington inherited some of his captives, and he acquired others through his marriage to Martha Washington, who was a widow.[117] Ona Maria Judge was born enslaved in June 1773. Her parents were Betty—a captive of George and Martha Washington—and Andrew Judge, an English-born white man who was an indentured servant in Virginia.[118] Judge was light skinned with freckles. She more than likely spent her childhood days playing with siblings and other enslaved children until she was called to serve Martha Washington at the mansion house at the age of ten.[119]

MAINTAINING ENSLAVEMENT AS PRESIDENT

George Washington, successful in helping secure the colonies' independence from the British crown, became president of the new

United States of America in 1789, and he had to live in the capital of the new country. This was first in New York, New York, and later in Philadelphia, Pennsylvania. Martha Washington joined her husband and that meant that Judge joined the pair, along with other enslaved persons. However, the Washingtons had a problem: enslavement was abolished in Pennsylvania. What did that mean for their enslaved captives? Would they be freed upon their arrival in Philadelphia?

The Difference with Chattel Enslavement

Chattel enslavement allowed for Black people of African descent—throughout the Diaspora—to be brought and sold forever because they were considered property, not people. This is the type of enslavement known to most Americans. While Americans may give white enslavers a pass because enslavement was common in human history, chattel enslavement was not common. Chattel enslavement was a unique creation of European colonial powers like England, Spain, and France.

In 1780, Pennsylvania passed the Gradual Abolition Act.[120] This act outlawed enslavement, but it also gradually emancipated any person who was enslaved in the state prior to the law. This meant that someone who was captured and enslaved would have to be freed over time. Yet with any law, there's always a loophole, and the Washingtons found it.

The law held that if an enslaved person lived in Pennsylvania for at least six months, even if they were first enslaved outside Pennsylvania, they could petition for their freedom. President Washington believed that some of his captives, specifically Judge, were exempt from this law because they were under the age of eighteen[121] and because he was forced to stay in Philadelphia because he was president.[122] But the president was wrong.

Presidents Who Enslaved Africans

George Washington isn't the only president to enslave Africans and/or people of African descent. According to History.com, at least twelve presidents enslaved people during their lives; eight of those presidents held Africans and/or people of African descent captive while in office. Those presidents, in addition to George Washington, are Thomas Jefferson, James Madison, James Monroe, Andrew Jackson, Martin Van Buren, William Henry Harrison, John Tyler, James K. Polk, Zachary Taylor, Andrew Johnson, and Ulysses S. Grant.

A GLITCH IN THE MATRIX

Once Martha Washington realized that her slaves could be freed if they stayed in Philadelphia for more than half a year, she devised a plan to rotate their captives to serve them in Philadelphia every six months. She would then send them back to Virginia and bring up another group (restarting their residency clock) while also attempting to keep knowledge of the law away from them.

If an excursion to Virginia proved too hard for the family to do, a quick trip to a neighboring state such as New Jersey served the same purpose.[123] Enslaved persons meant a level of financial security for their captors, and the Washingtons were on the brink of financial ruin. So, it was important that their captives stay captives and didn't learn about of the law. But word got out in the presidential mansion, and Judge became aware of the law.

ONA JUDGE'S INSPIRATION TO FLEE

Judge spent the next five years in Philadelphia with the Washingtons (rotating every six months to Virginia and back). She watched enslaved people free themselves and witnessed the formation of Black communities among the free Black population of the city.[124]

But what sparked the desire to test the law for herself was that the president decided not to run for a third term, so her time in Philadelphia would come to an end.

Also, if she returned to Virginia, the Washingtons planned to give her to their granddaughter as a wedding gift. Because of that, Judge decided to escape her captivity. She feared living with the Washingtons' granddaughter because she was known for having a temper and proving to be difficult. Also, the granddaughter's husband would have sex with nonwhite women (two of his three sons were born to an Indigenous woman he wasn't married to), and that posed the possibility of rape (being forced to have sex).

THE GREAT ESCAPE

Neither George Washington's signing the Fugitive Slave Act nor the difficulty of a woman escaping successfully (a man had an easier time) stopped her. The Fugitive Slave Act of 1793 was passed by Congress and it commanded that any enslaved person who escaped into another state or federal territory must be returned to their captor. This law was strengthened in 1850 with the addition of text saying that slaves couldn't have a trial with a jury or testify on their own behalf. Judge contacted a group of free Blacks who planned her escape. On May 21, 1796, twenty-two-year-old Judge slipped out of the executive mansion and disappeared into the community of free Blacks in Philadelphia while the Washingtons ate their supper.[125]

When they realized that Judge had fled, the Washingtons immediately attempted to get her back. They placed ads in the newspaper and offered a $10 reward for her return, no matter what the race of the person who found her was.[126] But Judge didn't remain in Philadelphia long. She fled that city for Portsmouth, New Hampshire, a city with three hundred sixty free Black people and virtually no enslaved persons. That's where she would meet and marry Jack Staines, a free Black sailor, with whom she had three children.[127]

George Washington, no longer president, pursued Judge until his death, but she always avoided his attempts. When asked by a reporter if she had regrets about leaving the Washingtons, Judge responded, "No, I am free, and have, I trust, been made a child of God."[128] Judge died a free woman on February 25, 1848.

CHAPTER 10

HAITI AND EL LIBERTADOR'S GREAT BETRAYAL

One of the most important events in modern history is the liberation of Saint-Domingue (now Haiti) from the French at the turn of the nineteenth century. What makes the formation and existence of Haiti so important is that it is a nation liberated by Africans for Africans and Black peoples by way of revolution and revolt against their colonial oppressors.

I learned in school, and maybe you did too, that the United States was the first modern democracy. But that's not the case. What my grade-school teachers left out or were unaware of was that the United States was intentionally formed as a nation in which some people were free (white people) and others were not (African people and their descendants). The United States wasn't a democracy but rather a slavocracy: a society ruled by enslavers or those who benefited from the institution of enslavement.

Haiti, however, was a democracy. Its formation established the first democracy in the Western Hemisphere: one where all people are free. Haiti not only was a democracy but it also fought to secure democracy throughout the West. That's what educators ought to teach.

How Haiti Got Its Name

The newly liberated African and their descendants gave their home the name used by the island's Indigenous Taino inhabitants, Hayti (meaning "land of high mountains"), as a tribute to them. Although spelled "Haiti" (the French spelling, adopted by the United States), Hayti was the spelling adopted by the Blacks in power after liberation. In Haitian Creole, the name is spelled "Ayiti."

FEARFUL OF A BLACK NATION

The Haitian Revolution scared the white power structure in the United States, because the success of that massive insurrection could encourage enslaved Africans and their descendants in the South to revolt. The presidential administrations of both George Washington and John Adams were fearful of a plot by the Haitian leader at the time, Pierre Dominic Toussaint, or "L'Ouverture," to invade the U.S. Southern states and Jamaica to incite an insurrection in both places.[129] The elite (a small group in a society that holds a lot of power) of the slaveholding U.S. republic were terrified of the meaning of Haitian independence, the end of enslavement, and reform of the society as a whole to become more equal.[130]

The inborn desire for freedom and the spirit of democracy led the Haitian struggle for self-rule and recognition, as well as Haiti's hostile approach toward enslaving countries and colonies of Europe. Haitians took this approach almost immediately, even while the fate of their freedom was unclear during their revolution. When it became a nation, Haiti actively supported Black liberation throughout the African Diaspora. These efforts included seizing slave ships transporting Africans, bringing them to Haiti and freedom, and—even more troubling for enslavers—influencing revolts of the enslaved.

The African Diaspora

The African or Black Diaspora is the voluntary and involuntary movement of Africans and their descendants to various parts of the world during the modern and premodern periods.[131] The African Diaspora is an organic, or natural, process involving movement from an ancestral land, settlement in new lands, and sometimes renewed movement and resettlement elsewhere.[132]

INFLUENCING REVOLTS IN THE U.S.

L'Ouverture did not follow through with his desire to invade the southern U.S. to liberate enslaved African people there; as a result, he hoped to gain favor with the U.S.[133] But it didn't stop the Haitian people from working to achieve Black liberation in the U.S. Given the frequent commerce between Haiti and the United States, Blacks from the U.S. serving as cooks and other servants aboard ships had traveled to and from seaports in Haiti and communicated with the people there.[134] Such communications, and the inspiration of the Haitian Revolution, helped facilitate the 1811 plot on New Orleans—a plot that never turned into an actual insurrection. The U.S. government believed this plan was a continuation of the Haitian Revolution on American soil.[135]

Other examples of Haitians influencing events surrounding Black liberation in the United States include inspiring soldiers and sailors at the Georgia-Florida border at the time of the Seminole Wars in 1818[136]; conspiring with Denmark Vesey and others in the plot to overtake Charleston, South Carolina, in 1822[137]; and inspiring the Southampton County, Virginia, rebellion of Nat Turner of 1831, with Haitian refugees settled in Southampton recalling the Haitian Revolution.[138] (See "The Seminole Wars and the Legend of John Horse" on page 87 for more about the Seminole wars and "Revolts of the Enslaved in the United States" on page 74 for more on revolts of the enslaved in the U.S.) These liberation efforts continued throughout the Diaspora, including assisting Black rebels in the Dominican Republic to defeat Spain[139] and aiding the South American liberator Simón Bolívar.

SIMÓN BOLÍVAR AND A PROMISE BROKEN

Simón Bolívar was born in 1783, into a rich Venezuelan family, and received an elite education. He inherited four haciendas (Spanish for "plantations"), two houses in Caracas (the current capital city of Venezuela), and numerous slaves—he was an enslaver of Africans.[140] However, he gave it all up for the cause of revolution, hoping to free slaves throughout Spanish America—including in what are now Venezuela, Colombia, Peru, and Bolivia (the nation named after him).[141] For this, Bolívar was known as El Libertador ("the Liberator") and the George Washington of South America. Yet he did not free enslaved Black people immediately.

In 1815, he faced problems in his struggle for a revolution. He suffered a humiliating defeat at the hands of the Spanish, and he retreated to Jamaica. There he wrote his famous "Jamaica Letter," requesting help from European powers, particularly Britain, in his liberation effort.[142] But he received little to no help and was chased out of Jamaica. He then traveled to Haiti, where he found support from the president at the time, Alexandre Pétion. Pétion offered Bolívar a thousand rifles, ammunition, and other supplies. He also provided hundreds of Haitian sailors and soldiers who had fought in the Haitian Revolution. This help was provided with the condition that Bolívar abolish slavery in South America when he founded a new republic, and Bolívar agreed.[143]

With the help of the Haitians, Bolívar defeated the Spanish and declared himself president of what are now Venezuela, Colombia, Peru, Bolivia, Ecuador, and Panama. After helping Bolívar liberate Blacks throughout South America, about a hundred brave Haitians boarded a vessel loaded with ammunition and tried to liberate enslaved Blacks on the island of Puerto Rico.[144] Sadly, Bolívar broke his promise to Pétion. Rather than wholly abolishing slavery, Bolívar sought to maintain Latin America's racial and class hierarchy so that white elites like himself would not fall to a so-called mulatto take-over leading to, what Bolívar called, a *pardocracia*.[145] A *pardocracia* in English means a Black- and biracially led republic.

Having seen what it meant for Black people to be truly free and have power in Haiti, Bolívar complained bitterly when his own Black and Indigenous generals launched a coup (an overthrow of the government) against his growing authoritarianism in 1828. He was very angry that they dared to "want absolute equality." As a warning to South America's Black and brown populations, he had

RESISTANCE STORIES *from* BLACK HISTORY *for* KIDS

the mixed-race leader of the failed coup, José Padilla, executed.[146] Bolívar ended up like George Washington in more ways than one: he not only liberated a colony from a country but also continued enslavement under his watch.

CHAPTER 11

THE FIRST BLACK PRESIDENT

The office of the presidency is often promoted as the most esteemed job anyone could have. When I was young, a few of my friends and I first said that we wanted to be president, but as I grew older, I realized that wasn't likely. This wasn't because we were incapable of being president but because we were Black. There had never been a Black president of the United States when I was growing up. Maybe if I had seen images of Black presidents around the world, I would have thought differently about a Black person becoming president of the United States.

But one day, it happened. A Black person, Barack Obama, was elected president of the United States. He'll go down in history as the first Black President of the United States of America. But he wasn't the first Black president in North America. The first Black president in North America was a Mexican named Vicente Guerrero.

Mexico's First Black Liberator

The title of Mexico's first Black liberator belongs to Gaspar Yanga. Yanga, from West Africa and then captured and sent to Mexico, escaped enslavement with a group of followers and fled to the mountains, where they established a community under Yanga's leadership. For forty years, the community was left alone until the Spanish government deemed it dangerous and attacked. After Yanga and his forces defeated the Spanish, the sides entered peace negotiations. In 1618, the Spanish recognized the community as a free Black settlement. Mexicans today still honor Yanga for his role in Mexican history on behalf of Black liberation.

THE EMERGENCE OF VICENTE GUERRERO

Vicente Guerrero lived from 1781 to 1831 and was known for fighting for the equality of all people, regardless of race.[147] His efforts on behalf of all races may be because Guerrero descended from enslaved Africans.[148] Historian Joel Augustus Rogers called Guerrero the George Washington and Abraham Lincoln of Mexico.[149] Although Mexican, Guerrero was of African descent; those in opposition to him insulted him because of his dark skin.[150] Nevertheless, Guerrero fought for the liberation of all Mexicans.

He served as a general in Mexico's fight for independence from Spain from 1815 to 1821, rising through the ranks to become the commander in chief of the Mexican rebel forces. With each victory in battle, Guerrero grew stronger. As a result of his efforts in battle, Mexico won its freedom from the Spanish in 1821. Guerrero envisioned a future Mexico built on majority rule by those of his African and Indigenous roots.[151] Therefore, the agreement between Mexico and Spain included Clause 12: "All inhabitants... without distinction of their European, African, or Indian origins are citizens... with full freedoms to pursue their livelihoods according to their merits and virtues."[152]

GUERRERO'S SHORT-TERM PRESIDENCY

Guerrero worked with those in power to secure the rights of all Mexicans, including assisting with the writing of the Mexican Constitution. In 1828, he ran for president as the "people's party" candidate[153] and was elected upon the resignation of then-president Manuel Gómez Pedraza. He officially took office on April 1, 1829.

Once in office, Guerrero reformed the tax code to tax the rich, and he expelled any remaining Spaniards in Mexico. But the most transformative policy change made by Guerrero happened on September 16, 1829, when he outlawed enslavement throughout Mexico. He was able to do this by taking advantage of the emergency war powers granted to him by the Mexican Congress in case of an attack by the Spanish.[154] Of his decision, Guerrero said Mexico's "disgraced inhabitants" would at last enjoy "their sacred, natural rights."[155]

The decision to outlaw enslavement had a ripple effect in the United States. The decree made Mexico a sanctuary for Black people fleeing from slave labor camps in the southwest U.S., mainly in Texas.[156] Most people think of the Underground Railroad flowing only north to Canada. However, Guerrero facilitated the Underground Railroad flowing south to Mexico as well. (See "Harriet Tubman: The Greatest American Who Ever Was" on page 110 for more on the Underground Railroad.) Sensing the possibility of finding freedom in Mexico, enslaved Black people from as far away as Florida escaped to Mexico.[157] This is the legacy of President Vicente Guerrero.

Three months after abolishing enslavement, Guerrero was driven from Mexico City and forced to wage a guerrilla war against a new government of his political enemies—mainly because of the abolition of enslavement.[158] Kidnapped by agents of the hostile government, he was executed in February 1831.[159]

FREDERICK DOUGLASS: WRESTLING WITH THE MASTER

Frederick Douglass is one of the greatest Americans who ever lived. He is known not only for being an abolitionist advocating for the end of enslavement but also for being a great speaker, writer, and thinker. I learned briefly about Douglass in grade school, but I learned so much more when I was in college.

I had to write a book review, selecting a book from a series of titles collected by our professor. Douglass's autobiography was the book I chose. I am glad that I did. I learned so much, including that he advocated for African people throughout the Diaspora, was a supporter of women's suffrage (the right to vote), and started a newspaper to further the cause of the end of enslavement.

Douglass was a friend to other people in the abolitionist movement for Black lives, including the abolitionist John Brown—the famous white who planned an insurrection of the enslaved, which failed—and Harriet Tubman, who led many enslaved Black people to freedom. So great an intellectual and thinker he was that many white people couldn't believe that Douglass had ever been enslaved. But, in fact, he had been.

Certainly, the story of his escape is a rousing one; an even more exciting story, however, is the event that helped give Douglass the courage to escape in the first place: a fight for his very life.

TIME IN BONDAGE

Douglass was born in 1817 as Frederick Augustus Washington Bailey. According to historian David Blight, Douglass's mother was enslaved and his father was their captor.[160] Douglass's autobiography explains that he changed his last name to Douglass at the suggestion of a friend and dropped both his middle names.[161] Around the age of six or seven, after his mother died, Douglass was held captive by Thomas and Lucretia Auld and served Thomas's brother, Hugh Auld, in Baltimore, Maryland.

Hugh's wife, Sophia Auld, began teaching Douglass how to read and write, much to the disappointment of Hugh Auld. He said, "Learning would *spoil* the best [n-word] in the world. Now, if you teach that [n-word] how to read, there would be no keeping him. It would forever unfit him to be a slave. He would at once become unmanageable, and of no value to his master."[162] So upon the advice of Hugh, Sophia stopped teaching Douglass.

Nevertheless, he managed to learn to both read and write during his seven years with them. When sent off on errands, Douglass would trade food with young white boys his age in exchange for lessons on reading and writing.[163] For Douglass, learning to read and write gave him the desire and notion of freedom. He believed that the power of knowledge could lead to achieving his liberation.

THE WRESTLING MATCH

Captors would sometimes rent out their enslaved captives for a fee to make extra money. Once back with Thomas and Lucretia Auld, Douglass was hired out to various "masters." One such man was named Edward Covey, a man with a reputation as a "slave breaker," meaning he was known for breaking the spirit of enslaved persons to the point of obtaining their complete obedience. He did this through violence, and he attempted to do so with Douglass, primarily through whipping him.

Douglass was whipped so much and so often that when Covey whipped him, his wounds hadn't healed from the previous whipping. Most times, for fear of the situation in which white men had all the power, Douglass never attempted to defend himself. But on one occasion, Douglass decided to fight back. While Douglass was tending to horses, Covey attempted to tie him up, but Douglass stopped him. Douglass described the event:

> As soon as I found what he was up to, I gave a sudden spring, and as I did so, he holding to my legs, I was brought sprawling on the stable floor. Mr. Covey seemed now to think he had me, and could do what he pleased; but at this moment—from whence came the spirit I don't know—I resolved to fight; and, suiting my action to the resolution, I seized Covey hard by the throat; and, as I did so, I rose. He held onto me, and I to him. My resistance was so entirely unexpected, that Covey seemed taken all aback. He trembled like a leaf... He asked me if I meant to persist in my resistance. I told him I did, come what might; that he had used me like a brute for six months, and that I was determined to be used so no longer... We were at it for nearly two hours. Covey at length let me go, puffing and blowing at a great rate, saying that if I had not resisted, he would not have whipped me half so much. The truth was that he had not whipped me at all. I considered him as getting entirely the worst end of the bargain; for he had drawn no blood from me, but I had from him. The whole six months afterwards, that I spent with Mr. Covey, he never laid the weight of his finger upon me in anger. He would occasionally say, he didn't want to get hold of me again. "No," thought I, "you need not; for you will come off worse than you did before."[164]

THE AFTERMATH

Working for Covey helped to break Douglass's spirit; that's just what Covey was known for. However, that moment of fighting back revived Douglass's sense of humanity and drive for freedom. Although striking a white man was dangerous, Douglass decided that if ever beaten, he'd have to be beaten to death because he would fight back to the death for his own defense. When Douglass fought Covey, he was sixteen years old.

What Douglass had done could have cost him his life. However, Covey did not turn in Douglass to the police—a common occurrence for an enslaved Black who raised his hand against a white person, no matter the circumstances. Douglass reasoned that was because to do so would threaten Covey's reputation as a slave breaker. In any case, Douglass moved on from Covey and stood strong with every captor until he took freedom into his own hands and escaped enslavement at the age of twenty.

CHAPTER 13

THE AFRICAN ALLIANCE THAT ALMOST WAS

I love the game of basketball. I love playing it and watching it, especially the NBA games. Because I grew up near Philadelphia, it's no surprise that I was a Philadelphia 76ers fan. I still cheer for my guys on the Sixers. But I was also a Kobe Bryant fan, so that meant that I cheered for the Los Angeles Lakers too although I'm not from there. Kobe was from Philly, and that's how I justified my fandom. I remember in 2011 when the New Orleans Hornets (now called the New Orleans Pelicans) were trading the Phoenix Suns point guard Chris Paul to the Lakers to play with Kobe. In my mind, Kobe and Chris would have made the best backcourt in the NBA at the time.

The trade almost happened, but in the end, the commissioner of the league vetoed it. Had the trade gone through, I believe the Lakers would have won more championships. It would have completely changed the landscape of the NBA. Of all the what-ifs in history, I use to think this was one of the biggest—that is, until I learned of a partnership that almost happened between the rulers of a few nations in the nineteenth century. Had these nations come together to accomplish what they intended, our world might be completely different from what it is today.

LIBERTY AND JUSTICE FOR ALL

When Vicente Guerrero was president of Mexico for just a few months in 1829, his focus was on not only creating a fair society for all Mexicans but also liberating Black people. (See "The First Black President" on page 52 for more on Vicente Guerrero.) He was a descendant of African people who were once enslaved, and he never wavered from the commitment to liberation.[165]

Therefore, he abolished enslavement throughout Mexico on September 16, 1829. But the enslaved Blacks in Mexico weren't his only concern. Guerrero thought about how he could use his power and position to free enslaved African people throughout the Diaspora and create a partnership of nations to counter slaveholding nations, such as England, Spain, France, and the United States of America.

THE PRESIDENT'S PLAN

Without informing the public or many in his administration, Guerrero secretly sent a representative to the Haitian capital Port-au-Prince to negotiate a treaty of alliance with then-president Jean-Pierre Boyer.[166] Guerrero wanted to partner with Haiti because just as the Mexican people had liberated themselves from Spain, Haiti was a nation of people who had liberated themselves from a colonial power, France. (See "L'Ouverture and the Taking of Saint-Domingue" on page 36 and "Haiti and El Libertador's Great Betrayal" on page 47 for more on the Haitian Revolution.) Also, Haiti, like Mexico, abolished enslavement and was led by Black people.

Those similar traits—liberation from colonial powers and ending enslavement—tied in with Guerrero's goals. Only a government that had enacted the most extreme antislavery policies would consider the plan Guerrero had in mind. He wanted Mexico and Haiti to invade Cuba and free the enslaved Blacks there.[167] Sadly, Guerrero's presidency lasted only months before he was driven out of office, so he couldn't help carry out his plan. But the negotiations between the Haitian and Mexican governments continued after Guerrero's departure and later death.

THE FATE OF THE PLOT

Even after Guerrero, Haiti remained interested in an alliance. At the time of the negotiations initiated by Guerrero, Haiti was occupying the Dominican Republic, named Santo Domingo at the time; the Haitians took control of the state from the Spanish. Hence, like Mexico, Haiti faced the anger of the Spanish, who threatened to invade both Mexico and Hispaniola to recapture its former colonies.

Cuba was related to all this because, like Mexico and the Dominican Republic, it was a Spanish colony. And the Cubans were looking to revolt. In Cuba, a secret society of Mexicans prepared for a revolution led by enslaved African people. The Spanish had heard that Haiti was preparing to send three thousand troops to assist the enslaved Blacks of Cuba with their revolt.[168] Guerrero's grand plan, which the governments of Mexico and Haiti continued to support, was to liberate Cuba and then establish an alliance of former colonies, which had enslaved Africans, that had become nations led by liberated Black people. This alliance would both protect against colonizing nations and liberate enslaved persons throughout the Western Hemisphere; this was a real threat to enslaving countries, including the United States.

But these nations never carried out the plan. U.S. Secretary of State Martin Van Buren promised Mexican officials that he would ensure that Spain recognized the sovereignty of Mexico in exchange for abandoning an alliance with Haiti to free enslaved Blacks in Cuba. As for the plan's goal, Van Buren stated that "the U.S. could never be [uninterested], seeing as they have so many [enslaved Black people] in the Southern states."[169]

CHAPTER 14

MAROON COMMUNITIES IN THE UNITED STATES

Of course, fleeing enslavement was an act of resistance, and several thousand enslaved people ran away from captivity. Exactly how many ran away? It depends on whom you ask, but no one knows for sure. Some scholars say that the best estimate is a range between twenty-five thousand and forty thousand. Others top that figure at fifty thousand.[170] The National Underground Railroad Freedom Center in Cincinnati, Ohio, says that the number could be as high as one hundred thousand.[171]

When I learned about formerly enslaved people running away, I mainly thought of Canada as their destination. I later learned that Mexico was another destination for the Underground Railroad. (See "The First Black President" on page 52 for more on the Underground Railroad in Mexico and "Harriet Tubman: The Greatest American Who Ever Was" on page 110 for more on the Underground Railroad in general.) However, a reality for some enslaved people was to remain within the borders of the United States. Was there a place to go and live out of harm's way of whites in the U.S. before the Civil War? Yes. Many enslaved persons escaped to Maroon communities throughout the South. When the Underground Railroad was not an option, marronage, or the act of liberating oneself from enslavement, was.

MAROONS IN THE UNITED STATES: A BACKGROUND

"Maroon" is a term used to describe a person who escaped slavery. African people established and maintained Maroon settlements throughout the Americas and the Caribbean. Maroon communities existed within territories that allowed enslavement, so these Black people were politically recognized, yet they couldn't vote. They were considered in political decisions though. These communities were common and very much a part of American life during the period of enslavement. These extremely effective sources of defiance offered a safe place for fugitives, served as bases for attacks on nearby plantations, and at times supplied the leadership for planned rebellions.[172]

Types of Marronage

Historians classify marronage into two general ways: intralimital and extralimital. Intralimital marronage involved people or groups fleeing to areas within the slavocracy—a place in which enslavement is the policy of the land. In this case, formerly enslaved people fled to areas within the United States, primarily in the South, either temporarily or permanently. Extralimital marronage involved people or groups fleeing to areas outside the U.S. to Canada, Mexico, or any noncolonial territory.[173]

Maroon settlements were often located in mountainous, forested, or swampy regions of South Carolina, North Carolina, Virginia, Louisiana, Florida, Georgia, Mississippi, and Alabama.[174] Evidence exists of at least fifty such communities in various places and at various times, from 1672 to 1865: the most notable communities were in the Great Dismal Swamp between Virginia and North Carolina. About two thousand fugitives, or the descendants of fugitives, likely lived in this area.[175] Captors of Blacks became aware of these communities primarily either when the activities of those within Maroon settlements threatened the slave establishment or when those Maroons became obnoxious, raiding plantations and attacking whites, for example. When these communities were discovered, enslavers sought to destroy them to prevent more from being established.

Understanding the Vocabulary

The word "maroon" first appeared in English in 1866. The word was taken from the French word *marron*, which means "runaway Black slave." A similar meaning applies to the Spanish *cimarrón*, which has additional meanings, including "wild runaway slave," "the beast who cannot be tamed," or "living on mountaintops."[176] It is important to note that most Africans did not refer to themselves as Maroons. They usually chose liberatory, powerful names such as "Nyankipong Pickibu," which means "children of the Almighty" in Twi, a language widely spoken in Ghana, West Africa.[177]

Militias, sometimes with the help of local Indigenous people, raided Maroon communities. Many were completely destroyed and Black men and women alike were killed. But some communities successfully maintained their independence for a long time, like those who fought alongside the Indigenous Black Seminole communities in northern Florida during the late 1700s and early 1800s against the so-called patriots seeking to take both their land and freedom.

What Is Drapetomania?

In 1851, physician Samuel A. Cartwright developed the term "drapetomania," considered a mental illness, to explain why enslaved Blacks ran away. It was defined (as late as 1914) as "an uncontrollable or insane impulsion to wander." To keep captives under control, Cartwright suggested using the Bible to keep captives enslaved while being kind, gracious, and meeting his [captives] physical needs to prevent captives from running away.[178]

MARRONAGE AND THE GREAT DISMAL SWAMP

The Great Dismal Swamp of North Carolina and Virginia was a remote landscape where many Black people, as well as Indigenous people, lived in the 225 years prior to the Civil War. This community came about due to a battle in which thousands of people rose up against the horrors of enslavement and escaped to the swamp for safety and to exercise their human rights.[179]

Most scholars agree that the swamp was home to the largest population of Maroons in North America in the eighteenth and nineteenth centuries. Between 1630 and 1865, thousands of Maroons, enslaved laborers, and excluded Indigenous people lived in this area and formed communities that were connected through a swamp-wide culture of existence.[180] Whites knew about these settlements and regularly shared information about them in newspapers and other media.

The attention to the Maroons of the Great Dismal Swamp occurred throughout American history. These times of focus on them specifically include the American Revolution from 1775 to 1783 and the famed rebellions of abolitionists Gabriel Prosser, Denmark Vesey, and Nat Turner.[181] (See "Revolts of the Enslaved in the United States" on page 74 for more about these men.) The Maroons and the Great Dismal Swamp got so much public attention that laws were enacted in North Carolina to allow for a class of captors and killers of Maroons to emerge to target Blacks and Indigenous peoples who lived in these communities.

Nevertheless, these communities thrived to the extent that in some cases the inhabitants knew others only from these settlements. A Great Dismal Swamp Maroon who eventually made his way to Canada said this about these remote-dwelling Maroons in an interview: "Dar is families growed up in dat dar Dismal Swamp dat never seed a white man, an' would be skeered most to def to see one. Some runaways went dere wid dar wives, an' dar childers ar raised dar."[182] Clearly, such Maroons intended on withdrawing from the outside world, and they most likely belonged. to the most self-reliant of all Maroon communities in the Great Dismal Swamp.[183]

CHAPTER 15

MAROON COMMUNITIES IN THE AFRICAN DIASPORA

Maroon communities existed not only in the United States but also throughout the Diaspora during the time of colonial enslavement. Maroon settlements existed throughout South America, Central America, and the Caribbean, most likely even before they did in the United States. The first such communities of Blacks sprung up in the Caribbean in as early as the start of the sixteenth century.

JAMAICA MAROONS

Jamaica is an island nation, the third largest in the Greater Antilles. It is commonly known now for its Olympic sprinters and reggae music, notably the music of the great Bob Marley. But this island nation made up of Black people of African descent should also be recognized for its history of resistance and rebellion.

The Kromanti

Jamaican Maroons called themselves Kromanti. The Kromanti were a subgroup of the people of Ghana who famously rose up together against a king in their homeland.[184] They were known for their military skills, and their Black descendants (the Jamaican people) prided themselves on using military skill to build Maroon communities and fight against colonial enslavers in numerous wars.

Africans, along with some remaining Indigenous people, established Maroon communities in response to Spanish rule. This immediately threatened the Spanish governance of the island, which lasted during the fifteenth and sixteenth centuries after Columbus claimed the island for the Spanish in 1494. Then the English invaded the island in the seventeenth century. Maroon communities resisted.

The Maroon resistance at the start of the British invasion prompted one Spanish commander to conclude that the Maroons were loyal to the Spanish.[185] However, the Maroons disproved that thought after establishing an alliance with the British to remove the remaining Spanish from the island.[186] Yet the Maroons and the British came into conflict themselves, primarily because the British enslaved Blacks, as they had done in their other colonies.

Despite the resulting decline of the Maroon population as a result of conflict with the British, the group posed a serious challenge to the English. This threat grew as the system of enslavement expanded and an increasing number of British-owned enslaved Blacks fled the plantations and joined existing Maroon communities.[187]

THE JAMAICAN MAROON WARS

Maroons from both the east and west sides of the island fought the British, and these battles were known as the Maroon Wars. After two exhausting wars (1720–1739 and 1795–1796), the British gave up and signed peace treaties with the Maroons in 1739 and 1796. These enabled the Maroons to remain free and self-governing until slavery was abolished in the British Commonwealth in 1834.[188]

Many consider Haiti's rebellion as the only successful mass revolt of the enslaved, and this is accurate because those Blacks were the only ones to establish a nation-state. But the Black people of African descent in Jamaica, specifically those of the Maroon territories, successfully achieved the power to govern themselves.

Some Maroon communities survived and exist to this day. They elect a council, led by a colonel or chief, to govern the people. Communities are typically crime-free, but residents are allowed to utilize Jamaica's judicial system (the branch of the government that deals with justice and contains the court system) if needed.[189] The Jamaican government, established in 1962 when British rule ended, has largely respected the centuries-old Maroon treaties.[190] Although the government does not collect taxes on Maroon lands, which cannot be sold or used for credit at a bank, it provides resources— roads, bridges, schools, and clinics, for example—for the four main surviving Maroon villages: Charles Town, Moore Town, Accompong Town, and Scott's Hall.[191]

QUILOMBO DOS PALMARES

As mentioned above, some of the more successful Maroon communities in the Diaspora existed in Jamaica. But maybe the most celebrated of all Maroon settlements throughout the Diaspora was Quilombo dos Palmares in Brazil. *Quilombo* is the Portuguese word for a Maroon community. The word *quilombo* is originally from Angola (in Africa) and refers to a military camp.[192]

While the Portuguese referred to the quilombo as Palmares, the people who lived there referred to the community as *Angola Janga*, or "Small Angola"; these communities of African descent became multiethnic over time.[193] What made Palmares so special was that it was a federation of Maroon towns, which means that these linked towns governed themselves yet also had a central authority to protect against a colonizer invasion.

Palmares lasted one hundred fifty years in colonial Brazil, with its population of runaway enslaved people, the enslaved, free persons captured in raids, and a large group of Indigenous women.[194] Palmares was the largest, best-defended, and best-organized Maroon community throughout all the Diaspora. Quilombos exist to the present day, and traces of Africa unquestionably live on in the Black diasporic cultures that resisted enslavement and oppression.[195]

ZUMBI OF PALMARES

The last leader of this community was Zumbi, also known as Zumbi of Palmares, who remains a powerful figure in Brazilian history. Before Zumbi became the leader, Palmares was ruled by Ganga

Zumba, who in 1677 signed a treaty with Portuguese leaders to end a war in which the Portuguese captured his family member. The treaty allowed Palmares to remain sovereign, with Ganga Zumba as its leader, in exchange for returning enslaved fugitives and moving the settlement to a different location.[196]

This didn't sit well with some within the federation, including Zumbi. Zumbi and his supporters rebelled and started an uprising against Ganga Zumba. They successfully poisoned Ganga Zumba, and Zumbi took the throne. Clearly, Ganga Zumba's agreement had created a division in Palmares, but his death may also be viewed as the widespread African practice of lawful regicide (the act of killing a king)—the severest penalty for royal weakness or abuse of power.[197]

As soon as Zumbi assumed power, the war restarted with new assaults on Palmares by the Portuguese. Zumbi and a band of his followers continued fighting the Portuguese for over a year until an aide revealed his location, and he and his men were killed in a surprise attack.[198] Palmares fell to the Portuguese at the end of the seventeenth century, and Zumbi was decapitated during the attack on Palmares.

For many Brazilians, especially those of African descent, Zumbi embodies the strongest resistance to slave-based colonial rule and, consequently, the struggle for economic and political justice today.[199] The Brazilian national holiday Dia da Consciência Negra (Black Awareness or Black Consciousness Day, established in 1978) is celebrated on November 20, the anniversary of Zumbi's execution by the Portuguese in 1695. It's also known as Zumbi Day.[200]

CHAPTER 16

NO NEW BABIES

When I was a kid, I counted my blessings that I wasn't born enslaved. Whenever learning about enslavement, I thought about the horrors of living as an enslaved person. I also thought about my parents and what it would mean to live enslaved with children, who were also enslaved. I can only imagine living with the fear that your child may be harmed, sold, or even killed. I was amazed that enslaved Blacks continued to have children under the conditions of enslavement. As I got older, I learned that wasn't true for everyone.

A DIFFERENT KIND OF RESISTANCE

Resistance during enslavement took many forms. One that often gets overlooked is the form of birth control, or contraception. Historians who have examined contraception among enslaved women generally view it as a form of resistance.[201] This topic is usually overlooked, probably because when discussing enslavement, like with many other topics of discussion, we often lump both sexes together rather than thinking specifically about the struggles women experienced as enslaved persons.

For example, their bodies were considered both pleasurable and profitable by their white male captors. Sadly, enslaved women could be raped (forced to have sex) by their captors or pressured into having sex upon the fear of physical violence or actual violence to a loved one. Additionally, after the shutdown in 1808 of U.S. trade that delivered Africans to be enslaved, enslaved women could be treated as literal baby factories for producing new enslaved people.

Captors of enslaved persons decided to "breed" their enslaved captives, as they might breed livestock, to replenish the number of enslaved persons or to create a new way to make more money.

Sojourner Truth, in her famous speech "Ain't I a Woman," shared the pain of that happening to her on a plantation: "I have borne thirteen children and seen most all sold off to slavery, and when I cried out with my mother's grief, none but Jesus heard me! And ain't I a woman?"[202] Rather than deal with that grief, or let their captors be enriched by the enslaved women producing babies, some women chose to resist with what we'd consider unusual ways to prevent pregnancy.

METHODS OF CONTRACEPTION

Birth control was looked down upon in most Western countries, at least from the start of Christianity until the middle of the twentieth century.[203] Even today it is disliked by certain religious groups. But opposition to birth control never stopped women from exercising their ability to practice it. Birth control in the United States during the antebellum period, the time from the early to mid-1800s,[204] looked very different from what it does today. ("Antebellum" means before the Civil War. This period, where enslavement was the law of the land, existed at the formal start of the United States until the Civil War.) Today, you can generally go to your local pharmacy and purchase contraceptives (types of birth control). That was not the case during the nineteenth century.

Enslaved women, and women in general, would use oral (taken by mouth) contraceptives, including the mineral calomel and the oil turpentine. Once manufacturers of turpentine became aware of this practice among enslaved women, they changed the recipe to make turpentine useless as birth control.[205] But enslaved women had different means to achieve their goal.

They relied on their knowledge from Africa[206] of using nature as a mode of contraception. Among Mandingo women, the root of the cotton tree, which grew in abundance in parts of Africa, was used to end pregnancies.[207] (Liese Perrin, in "Resisting Reproduction," observes: "Although it is generally thought that African societies did not encourage birth limitation, it was practiced—for reasons including conceiving under unsuitable circumstances.") Having passed down knowledge of medicine and oral (spoken) traditions, enslaved women were able to adapt in the new environment of the American South and apply what they knew.

COTTON ROOT

In parts of Africa, wild cotton plants grow, but the main source of cotton was from cotton trees, which are much bigger than the cotton plants in America.[208] Despite this difference in appearance, when enslaved women found themselves knee-deep in the cotton fields of the American South, it was not difficult for them to recognize the plant and continue using cotton roots as a natural form of birth control.[209] From accounts shared by formerly enslaved persons, we know that cotton root was used as natural contraceptive and that the practice was a form of resistance.

Mary Gaffney, a formerly enslaved woman in Texas who shared her account of her resistance, gave an example. Her captor forced her to marry a man she didn't love, so she refused to have sex with him. Her husband complained to her captor, and Mary was whipped to force her to have sex with the man she married against her will. Not wanting to have children with him, she used cotton root to resist. Gaffney said, "Maser was going to raise him a lot more slaves, but still I cheated Maser, I never did have any slaves to grow and Maser he wondered what was the matter. I tell you son, I kept cotton roots and chewed them all the time but I was careful not to let Maser know or catch me."

The ignorance of captors had them believe that these women who used cotton root were unable to have children. But after the Civil War ended in 1865, the birthrate among Black people rose, whereas it had declined between 1830 and 1860. Once free, formerly enslaved women, including Gaffney, who had used cotton root, went on to have several healthy children.

BY THE NUMBERS: THE ECONOMICS OF ENSLAVEMENT*

$800
The cost of an enslaved African American in 1860

$28,160.40
The hypothetical cost of an enslaved African American in 2020

$196,000
Relative income of an unskilled enslaved person in 2020

400%
Increase in cotton picked per day by the enslaved, 1800–1860

$30
Annual cost to take care of an enslaved person in 1860

$1,056
The hypothetical annual cost to take care of an enslaved person in 2020

$4 BILLION
The total wealth held by enslaved persons in 1860

$42 TRILLION
The total wealth held by enslaved persons in 2020 dollars

13,000
Enslaved persons accepted as collateral by J.P. Morgan bank

* Catarina Saraiva, "Four Numbers That Show the Cost of Slavery on Black Wealth Today," *Bloomberg* (March 2021), https://www.bloomberg.com/news/articles/2021-03-18/pay-check-podcast-episode -2-how-much-did-slavery-in-u-s-cost-black-wealth?leadSource=uverify%20wall.

Samuel Williamson and Louis Cain, "Measuring Slavery in 2020 Dollars," MeasuringWorth.com, last accessed November 14, 2022, https://www.measuringworth.com/slavery.php.

Sven Beckert and Mark Stelzner, "The Contribution of Enslaved Workers to Output and Growth in the Antebellum United States," Washington Center for Equitable Growth, June 24, 2021, page 15, https:// equitablegrowth.org/working-papers/the-contribution-of-enslaved-workers-to-output-and-growth -in-the-antebellum-united-states.

P. R. Lockhart, "How Slavery Became America's First Big Business," *Vox* (August 2019), https://www .vox.com/identities/2019/8/16/20806069/slavery-economy-capitalism-violence-cotton-edward -baptist.

Clyde Ford, "Founding Fathers as Founding Debtors: How Some of Them Used Slaves as Collateral," *LA Times* (July 2021), https://www.latimes.com/opinion/story/2021-07-01/founding-fathers-july -fourth-slaves.

CHAPTER 17

REVOLTS OF THE ENSLAVED IN THE UNITED STATES

In college, I had the opportunity to take the course "African American Culture." One day, we were having a conversation about Independence Day celebrations. My professor, Katrina Hazzard-Donald, said that such celebrations in Western societies[210] center on revolution—when the people revolt against the political order or those in political power. (Western societies are those in Europe, North America, Central America, South America, Australia, and the Caribbean.) Generally, those in power won't give up their power without a fight. Thus, with revolution comes bloodshed by people fighting to achieve their liberation.

Hazzard-Donald referenced the French and American revolutions as examples to make the point that Black people are without an Independence Day in the traditional sense: our freedom from enslavement was the freedom to be citizens within a white settler colonial project rather than liberation from a white settler colonial project. Much of that has to do with the racial makeup of the United States; unlike countries in the Caribbean and parts of South America, Black people never outnumbered white people.

Therefore, enslaved people in the United States didn't have the same circumstances—being in the majority—to take out a colonial power like the Haitians did with the French. But what is true is that Black people enacted their own revolutions long before President Abraham Lincoln issued the Emancipation Proclamation, and their liberation often came at the cost of their captors' blood.

REVOLT AS RESISTANCE

Revolt was just one form of resistance by enslaved Black people.[211] According to historian Herbert Aptheker, enslaved African people's resistance against their enslavement took eight forms: purchasing freedom; strikes; sabotage; suicide and self-mutilation; flight (running away); enlisting in the armed forces; anti-enslavement agitation in speaking and writing; and revolts. Revolts, said Aptheker, were the result of three factors: economic hardship; unusual excitement about enslavement, that is, some kind of war; and large additions to the enslaved population.

Because of the vast number of revolts by enslaved people, people aren't expected to have heard about them all, let alone celebrate them. Just the mention of these revolts may be interpreted as a celebration of Black violence against white people. But revolts are an act of striving to reacquire the freedom all people have the right to have.

Students learn that freedom for the enslaved came by way of the voice of abolitionists and the goodwill of the federal government.[212] According to a Southern Poverty Law Center report, "Teaching Hard History," American public-school students have a distorted if not severely incomplete understanding of enslavement, its impact on America's economic history, and resistance to it by enslaved Black people. Students are aware of only so much about enslavement.

The truth is that enslaved Black people had much to do with achieving their own freedom. According to Aptheker, there are records of approximately two hundred fifty revolts and conspiracies in the history of Black enslavement in the United States.[213] White captors were so concerned about enslaved Africans revolting that laws were created to prevent the assembly of the enslaved. The U.S. Constitution included provisions to prevent insurrections of any kind, including insurrections among enslaved people.[214] Article 1, Section 8, Clause 15 of the U.S. Constitution states that Congress has the power to "provide for calling forth the Militia to execute the Laws of the Union, suppress Insurrections and repel Invasions."

The U.S. Constitution also governed enslavement in three additional clauses, including the importation clause (ending transport of Africans to the U.S. in 1808), the three-fifths clause (regarding African peoples as three-fifths of a person for political purposes), and the enslaved fugitive clause (demanding the return of any escaped enslaved person back to its legal captor).

FAMOUS REVOLTS

The most famous revolt of enslaved Blacks in U.S. history was led by Nat Turner. Turner's insurrection took place in Southampton County, Virginia, on August 22, 1831. Turner, a Christian minister, received prophetic visions and led roughly seventy enslaved Blacks on a rebellion to slaughter the white captors who enslaved them. This resulted in the slayings of fifty to sixty white people, including Turner's captors. Many of the rebels were captured by the local white militia, whereas Turner went into hiding for six weeks until his capture. Turner was tried, convicted, and hanged for leading the rebellion at the age of thirty-one.

Two of the most famous revolts almost occurred but never did: Gabriel Prosser's and Denmark Vesey's rebellions. Prosser was the twenty-four-year-old leader of an unsuccessful insurrection in Richmond, Virginia. He organized hundreds of people to fight and kill all whites on August 30, 1800. However, two enslaved people informed their captor, then-Governor (and fifth U.S. president) James Monroe of the plot. Prosser was captured, tried, and executed.

Vesey was a free Black man and Christian pastor in Charleston, South Carolina. Vesey's rebellion, planned for June 1822, involved freeing hundreds of enslaved Blacks and leaving for Haiti with the help of both free and enslaved Blacks. But the revolt was betrayed by two enslaved people. Vesey was captured, tried, and executed at fifty-five years old.

MORE REVOLTS

Sadly, it's safe to assume that students know very little about revolts of the enslaved. What may be known are plots and revolts of the few, like the rebellions mentioned above. But so much more is unknown. Here are some brief examples of lesser-known revolts or conspiracies. While the list below is only a brief example of revolts, it can serve as an introduction to a history rarely spoken of:[215]

The Stono Rebellion of 1739 was an event in which twenty enslaved Blacks broke into a South Carolina store on the Stono River Bridge, stole firearms, and killed the owner. They marched through Georgia and recruited other enslaved Blacks while killing whites on their way to Spanish Florida and their freedom. When confronted by the English, the Blacks held them off for seven days before the English killed most of the rebels.

The Cane River Insurrection of 1804 began when a group of nine enslaved Blacks departed from the Cane River plantation in Natchitoches Parish, Louisiana, for Tejas (Texas) in Spanish Mexico with ammunition and horses. However, at the request of one of the captors, Mexican authorities returned the Blacks to him in Louisiana.

The Camden, South Carolina, Slave Conspiracy of 1816 was designed to create a diversion to distract the whites in one area of Camden so enslaved Blacks could kill whites in other areas, eventually to kill them all and set fire to the town. The conspiracy was betrayed by a domestic enslaved person because of his unwillingness to leave the area or the service of his captor.

The Ohio River Revolt of 1826 occurred when seventy enslaved Blacks who were being transported by boat to be sold in the deep South broke out of confinement and killed the five white men on the ship with various weapons found onboard. After taking money and weapons, the enslaved men sank the boat and attempted to reach Indiana, but they were captured. Some were executed and others were sold back into enslavement.

The Christiana Resistance of 1851 was led by William and Eliza Parker, who had escaped enslavement, along with a group of Black community members. They defended four escaped enslaved Black people, originally from Maryland, from slave catchers in Christiana, Pennsylvania, killing the captor of those four enslaved people. William Parker fled upon the arrival of authorities. With the help of Frederick Douglass, William arrived in Canada. His wife, Eliza, joined him months later.

CHAPTER 18

REVOLTS OF THE ENSLAVED THROUGHOUT THE DIASPORA

In schools in the United States, Black history is often taught without providing the context of Black history throughout the African Diaspora. But Black people existed all over the world—for example, in Brazil (Afro-Brazilians), Mexico (Afro-Mexicans), the United States (Afro-Americans), and many other countries in the Western Hemisphere. They had ties to enslaved Black people and were aware of their struggles for freedom.

What Is a Social Construct?

It may be confusing, for example, to know the difference between "Black" and "African American" or "Afro-Mexican." The latter two terms are ethnic or cultural identifiers, whereas the term "Black," like "white," is a social construct. That means that "Black," like "white," has meaning because people have created and agreed on that meaning. But over time, being categorized as "Black" or "white" has real-life consequences due to the history of oppression and privilege as a result of racism. Whether one is Black or white can determine if one can purchase a home, the quality of one's school, and how one is treated when confronted by police.

LIBERATION LOOKS DIFFERENT OUTSIDE THE U.S.

Black people throughout the Diaspora, with the exception of those in the United States, generally identify with the nation where they achieved liberation from its colonial overlords because of how that freedom was achieved. For example, in Mexico, Haiti, and numerous countries in South America, this hard-won freedom in becoming a liberated territory was a group effort of all races of people and was often led by Black people. They emancipated themselves from a colonial power and enslavement was abolished.

People in the United States, however, emancipated themselves from a colonial power—Great Britain—during the Revolutionary War, but the war was not a group effort of whites and Blacks through which enslavement was abolished. Instead, Black people chose to fight on either side (for the colonies or the British) to earn their personal freedom. Once emancipated by way of the Civil War, Black people remained under the authority of their oppressor—white Americans—unlike emancipated Black people throughout the Diaspora who had started their own governments.

With that said, all Black people throughout the Diaspora drew inspiration from one another in their quests for liberation. Black people in the United States never saw themselves apart from other Black people throughout the Diaspora; they saw themselves as all victims of white settler colonialism. Black people of the United States were invested in and supportive of Black liberation movements throughout the Western Hemisphere, including those in Haiti, Mexico, and Cuba.[216]

SOME FAMOUS REVOLTS THROUGHOUT THE DIASPORA

The Haitian Revolution (1791–1804) is the most successful revolt of enslaved Africans, which led to the creation of the first independent Black nation in the Western Hemisphere. (See "L'Ouverture and the Taking of Saint-Domingue" on page 36 for more information about the Haitian Revolution.) But there were countless other revolts and conspiracies in history against white settler colonialism that happened outside the North American continent of which little is known. Below is a list of some of those revolts and conspiracies.

(For more information, refer to the *Encyclopedia of Slave Resistance and Rebellion*, edited by Junius P. Rodriguez.)

The Puerto Rico Revolt of 1527 was a major rebellion of enslaved Africans and Indigenous peoples, although it was brief. Those who escaped fled to the mountains and lived in Maroon communities with the Taino people.[217] (According to University of Wisconsin Professor Michael P. Gueno, the name "Taino" came into common usage in the twentieth century, and "Taino" was assigned by historians and anthropologist to refer to the entire Indigenous population of western Caribbean peoples; the correct names for the Indigenous people of this region are the Arawak of the Greater Antilles and the Carib of the Lower Antilles.) Such rebellions continued to happen in Puerto Rico until enslavement was abolished in 1873.

During the St. Kitts Rebellion of 1639, sixty enslaved Africans, including women and children, ran away from their brutal captors to retreat to the mountains. They tried to defend themselves, but the rebellion was put to an end. One Black man was able to escape and mount attacks on French captors for three years, receiving information from enslaved peoples, until he was killed.

Tacky's Rebellion of 1760–1761 was one of the most serious insurrections of enslaved Africans in Jamaican history. Named after an overseer named Tacky, the rebellion began on Easter Sunday in 1760 and lasted for six months, with thousands of enslaved people joining and carrying out a guerrilla-like revolt. When the rebellion was eventually suppressed, most rebels chose to commit suicide rather than return to enslavement.

Bussa's Rebellion of 1816 was the longest armed rebellion in the history of Barbados (involving four thousand to five thousand enslaved rebels), led by Bussa, an African-born person captured and shipped to this island to work on a sugar plantation. A major organizer of the rebellion was an enslaved African woman, Nanny Grigg. Like Tacky's Rebellion, this one also started on Easter Sunday, because this was a time of celebration and merriment, when whites would let their guard down. Although the rebellion was put down in five days, with the killing of Bussa, the fighting didn't end until several months later.

The St. Croix Rebellion of 1848 was a major uprising of enslaved Africans, resulting in their emancipation from two centuries of rule by Denmark.

CHAPTER 19

WHITE WARS AND BLACK LIVES

Whenever teachers in school taught about the wars involving the United States, of course the United States was painted as the hero. Black people, I was taught, fought on the side of the U.S. in just about every war. Since Black people never fought with the "enemy," it led me to believe that the U.S. always fought with Black people in mind. The truth is that in most cases, neither the United States nor its opponents were friends of Black people.

But Black people used wars involving the U.S. and its opponents to gain their freedom in some way. Choosing sides in a war wasn't about one side being right and the other being wrong. It was about choosing who would help Black people be free after the war.

WARTIME SUPPORT

Wars during the founding and early years of the United States were fought for the sovereignty and expansion of the new nation. The fighting was generally between white people—the Americans and the British—to protect the interests of Americans on their own soil. However, Black people had a role to play in these wars.

Their role resembled that of the Americans who were seeking to obtain and maintain the sovereignty of the land. But Black people in the United States wanted to obtain and maintain the sovereignty of their bodies. Whereas the British and the Americans had clearly defined sides, Black people stood on the side of Black freedom, and whites took advantage of this desire for freedom. Black people cleverly used their wartime support for whichever side secured their personal freedom.

You might say that the Civil War is an example of Black people choosing a side. However, the sides were clear, enslavement or emancipation. But consider the Revolutionary War or the War of

1812—wars in which Black liberation wasn't on the agenda, but it was something that could be gained by supporting a certain side. Wartime support was about an opportunity to weaken the oppressor and take advantage of a chance for freedom.

Diasporic Africans and American Wars

In the Revolutionary War, two Black units from abroad—from France and Spain—made significant contributions. The French unit was the West Indian Volunteer Chasseurs from Hispaniola, a unit of three thousand six hundred, of which six hundred men were of African descent. The Spanish unit was comprised of the troops of Bernardo de Galvez, a unit of seven hundred fifty, of which one hundred were of African descent.

BLACK SOLDIERS AND THE REVOLUTIONARY WAR

The Revolutionary War (also known as the American Revolution) in the United States took place from 1775 to 1783. White colonial settlers were fighting against Great Britain, the colonial power in charge of the thirteen colonies, for freedom. It is often taught that the English king's abuse of power was the reason for the Revolutionary War. The truth is that the war had more to do with colonial settlers' desire to enslave Blacks as Great Britain was abandoning the practice. (See "The Birth of a Nation" on page 33 for more about the roots of the Revolutionary War.)

During the war, enslaved Blacks fought alongside the British in exchange for their freedom. They took advantage of the fears of the British that more British soldiers wouldn't be readily available; the enslaved also realized that they couldn't secure a similar guarantee of freedom from the colonists because, at first, Blacks weren't allowed to fight alongside them.

In 1775, Lord Dunmore, the royal governor of Virginia, invited all rebel-owned, enslaved men to join the British side, and those who joined were promised their freedom.[218] Twenty-five thousand in South Carolina and nearly all enslaved people in Georgia fled from their captors to join the British. As for fighting with the "patriots," Blacks joined the patriot cause at first, until at the Council of War on October 8, 1775, General George Washington and others all voted to reject enslaved persons and a great majority voted to reject Africans altogether—whether free or enslaved.[219]

Washington specifically ordered, "Neither Negroes, boys, nor old men unable to bear arms, should be enlisted."[220] Thus, those who could escape to fight with the British did, including those Washington himself enslaved. Taking advantage of the war, Blacks also attempted to gain freedom by other means. They demanded their freedom, ran away, engaged in conspiracies, and even took part in armed attack, in which whole families of captors were wiped out.[221]

As a result, Washington changed course and allowed Blacks, particularly enslaved Blacks, to join the war in exchange for their emancipation. Once allowed to serve as soldiers, spies, and other roles of support, the tide of the war turned, and the rest is history. As for those who fought alongside the British, if they survived the war, they traveled with the British and settled in places throughout the British Empire or in West Africa.

BLACK SOLDIERS AND THE WAR OF 1812

Another example of Blacks in the United States selecting sides for their freedom happened during the War of 1812. This war between the U.S. and Great Britain was fought over shipping rights and the right for the U.S. to expand westward. During the war, nearly four thousand enslaved Africans took their freedom; nearly one-quarter of these enslaved persons pursued their fight for freedom while bearing arms against ex-masters alongside their British liberators.[222] However, if caught by Americans, they could and would be executed. Enslaved Blacks exploited the British invasion of the United States just as the British exploited the Black desire for freedom.[223]

Even Maroon communities, specifically those in South Carolina, Georgia, and Florida, joined the British to fight for Black freedom—freedom in exchange for fighting against the United States. They believed that with the support of ammunition from the British, Southern states could become their own republics, like Haiti in the Caribbean, because of the sizable populations of enslaved Blacks. With the hope of liberation and possible self-governance, it made sense for enslaved people to fight against their captors.

Yet some African Americans did fight with the United States because they believed that their continuing participation in the defense of the United States would result in gaining the freedom and rights of other citizens—that is, white people.[224] But at first, the U.S. War Department chose to follow the lead of the majority of states, excluding Black people from regular military service.[225]

Because the Marine Corps and Army didn't need any more soldiers, this did not affect them. But it was a problem for the Navy until 1813, when it was allowed to recruit Blacks to its forces. Blacks hurried to enlist and accounted for between 10 percent and 20 percent of the entire Navy during the war.[226] The role of Black soldiers on land was limited during the first years of the war, but by the later years, Blacks had participated in major land battles, specifically in New York state, Philadelphia, and New Orleans.

When the fighting ended with the Treaty of Ghent in 1814, those fighting alongside the United States, namely in Louisiana, earned their freedom. Enslaved persons fighting with the British who survived the war traveled with the British and settled throughout the British Empire as refugees.

Of course, the U.S. government demanded that the British return enslaved refugees, but they refused. An eleven-year negotiation ensued, and as a result, in 1826, Britain agreed to pay money to the former captors of those once-enslaved Blacks, in the amount of $1,204,960. The U.S. government and the British Parliament (similar to the U.S. Congress) agreed that the payment should go to the formerly enslaved rather than their captors.[227]

CHAPTER 20

THE SEMINOLE WARS AND THE LEGEND OF JOHN HORSE

Growing up, my favorite football team wasn't any team in the NFL. It was a college football team, the Florida State Seminoles. I remember watching quarterback Charlie Ward and running back Warrick Dunn lead the team to a national championship in 1993 at the Orange Bowl. Since my birthstone (garnet) is part of the team's colors, I fell in love with the team immediately. During the next season, I learned that a Seminole was an Indigenous person. I learned this after watching the team tradition of Chief Osceola planting a flaming spear adorned with Seminole feathers at the fifty-yard line during a game.

It's a tradition that continues today, and that is only because the university has the permission of the Seminole Tribe of Florida to do so.[228] Professional sports teams, including the Cleveland Guardians and the Washington Commanders, have recently changed their names from ones that offended Indigenous people. But due to Florida State's relationship with the Seminole Tribe, the tradition continues. The university works with the tribe to educate people on the history of the Seminole people—a history that includes Black Seminoles.

Where Is the Name "Seminole" From?

The word "Seminole" first appears in a 1765 English document referring to a band of Native Americans and originating from the Spanish word *cimarrón*.[229] Native Americans adopted it as Simaloni, and it evolved into Semanoli, and finally into Seminole. This group of Indigenous people took the term "Seminole" for identification by the beginning of the nineteenth century.[230] The term refers to the concept of people who run away, for example, removing themselves from populous towns and living by themselves.[231]

THE BLACK SEMINOLES

The Seminoles are an Indigenous people who were the first people of Florida, with their ancestors arriving over fourteen thousand years ago. The tribe developed through ethnogenesis, which means it formed through a coming together of various Indigenous groups. The Seminole Tribe began as a mixture the Hitchiti, Yuchi, Yamassee, and Apalachee tribes. Later, the Creek and Muskhogean tribes migrated into the territory and eventually mixed with these other groups.[232]

Black Seminoles resulted from enslaved Blacks escaping from captivity in Georgia, the Carolinas, and Florida to the Seminole territories. Black cohabitation with the Seminoles began shortly after the Seminoles formed as a united group of Indigenous tribes.[233] The Seminoles welcomed runaways. In time, when the Spanish took control of Florida from the British at the end of the American Revolution in 1783, Seminoles began to actively accept Blacks in the north Florida region so Black people could live freely.[234]

The escapees put themselves under the protection of the chiefs and in return provided services, including acting as interpreters for the whites and the Indigenous people. With their knowledge of the whites' ways and language, these escapees often developed into advisers for the tribes.[235] By 1812, several hundred Blacks from the Carolinas and Georgia who had escaped capture lived in Seminole Black towns, which naturally irritated white captors of Blacks who lived near those areas.[236]

THE FIRST SEMINOLE WAR

The unofficial start of the First Seminole War was in 1812 with the attempt of Georgia "patriots" to seize Saint Augustine, Florida, in the hopes of recapturing Blacks lost to escape and possibly taking Florida for the U.S. They did not succeed, as the Black people of Saint Augustine evaded capture. Another attack by the Georgia militia, this time in the Alachua towns of the Seminoles, was defeated by both Black and Indigenous Seminoles later that year. But in early 1813, U.S. troops were victorious in the region. This was a setback and not a defeat for Black and Indigenous Seminoles though, whose resistance prevented Florida—and their freedom—from being taken by the U.S.

The official start of the war was in 1817 with the U.S. attack on Fowl Town in Georgia after a local chief, Inihamathla, warned the leaders of nearby Fort Scott not to cross into tribal territory. Seminoles and Blacks retaliated by attacking a boat and taking control of five boats until U.S. troops got them back. Also, Blacks and Indigenous people raided plantations, freeing Black captives and killing settlers. When word of these hostilities got out, General Andrew Jackson was transferred to Fort Scott to crush the fighting and invade Florida.

In April 1818, Jackson, with the support of a Tennessee militia regiment and Creek Indigenous warriors, marched into Florida and pushed toward the town of Suwanee, with its Black and Indigenous villages. The Black and Indigenous Seminoles were outnumbered: four thousand eight hundred troops to one thousand local fighters.[237] The Battle of Suwanee ended with few Seminoles being killed or captured, yet the Black and Indigenous Seminoles did retreat deeper into the woods and swamps. Numerous Blacks and Indigenous people in lower Georgia and the Florida area reorganized and founded new towns, even as Florida became part of the U.S. in 1821.

JOHN HORSE AND THE SECOND SEMINOLE WAR

John Horse, whose given name was Juan Cavallo, was the son of a mixed-heritage (Spanish and Indigenous) Seminole trading man and his Black captive woman.[238] As a child, John Horse was a skinny kid who was intelligent, knowledgeable, and sly, tricking U.S. officers into purchasing multiple turtles, which were the same turtles he stole from them each night. This earned him the nickname "Gopher John," with "gopher" meaning "turtle."[239] As an adult, John Horse was six feet tall, strong, and recklessly brave. He became a fierce leader of a desperate, hard-fighting band of the formerly enslaved and Black Seminoles, who would play a key role in inflicting upon the proud Fourth United States Infantry its worst beating on the battlefield in eleven years.[240]

On a cool winter morning on December 28, 1835, John Horse was part of a group of hidden Indigenous people and Blacks who wiped out a one-hundred-five-man military unit from Fort Brooke in Florida. This attack shocked the entire country, sparking the Second Seminole War.[241] By late 1837, because of his victories in battles that began with the 1835 battle, John Horse had become the most feared and capable Black military leader in the Seminole nation.[242]

In addition to being a fierce warrior and agitator against the U.S. government, John Horse could fluently speak Seminole, Spanish, and the Black dialect of the formerly enslaved people from plantations. He mastered the art of being a tribal doctor and he was a skilled marksman (expert at shooting). He wore a cloth around his head with two or three big feathers in it to signify his Seminole heritage.[243] His desire to fight to the death to maintain his freedom signified both his Seminole and African heritages.

That fight suffered a setback when John Horse and another Black Seminole, Wildcat, were captured. Although they escaped, their imprisonment harmed the struggle because in their absence was an absence of their leadership. Much of John Horse's homeland had been overrun by U.S. troops, so he and others pushed further south to reorganize the resistance. The Battle of Lake Okeechobee

RESISTANCE STORIES *from* BLACK HISTORY *for* KIDS

on Christmas 1837 was the bloodiest contest of the Seminole Wars and a loss for the Seminole warriors, although John Horse's brave fighting made it his finest day in battle.[244]

After the battle, John Horse and his followers fled south with the Seminoles toward the last safe hideaway in the Florida Everglades, where they found a brief sanctuary.[245] However, life on the run resulted in the starvation and surrender of many. Since John Horse was worried about the survival of his own wife and children and as further resistance collapsed around him, he finally surrendered during the spring of 1838, ending his brave struggle for freedom.[246] By the summer of 1838, John Horse and his people had been transported by United States soldiers to the Indian Territory in what is now Oklahoma.[247] Their transport was part of the Trail of Tears.

The Second Seminole War lasted from December 1835 to August 1842, costing over $40 million and the lives of approximately fifteen hundred U.S. soldiers, in addition to the lives of white settlers and militiamen.[248] It is usually referred to as the country's longest-lasting and most expensive Indigenous war, but Major General Thomas Sidney Jessup—who was in command in Florida during the most crucial period of the war—announced late in 1836, "This... is a negro, not an Indian war."[249] That has everything to do with the power and determination of the Black Seminoles and their warrior chief, John Horse.

CHAPTER 21

GREAT ESCAPES DURING THE ANTEBELLUM

There are numerous tales of people who escaped enslavement during the antebellum period before the Civil War from around 1815 to 1861.[250] I had the good fortune of learning about these stories as a kid, and they reminded me that few things are stronger and more courageous than the human spirit, particularly when striving for one's freedom and the freedom of loved ones. These stories of escape are perfect examples of bravery in the face of grave danger.

ESCAPING IN A BOX

Henry "Box" Brown was born enslaved in Virginia in 1815. As a child, he was separated from his mother and family by his captor, who gifted the enslaved Brown to his son. As an adult, Brown was married and had three children. Brown and his wife, Nancy, had different captors, and due to the financial ruin of his wife's captor, she and her children were sold away. Nancy was pregnant with their fourth child.

Brown tried to catch them at the auction block, but he was too late. He would never see his family again. In an account, Brown shared his pain, saying, "My agony was now complete, she with whom I had traveled the journey of life in chains... and the dear little pledges God had given us I could see plainly must now be separated from me forever, and I must continue, desolate and alone, to drag my chains through the world."[251]

Although in despair, Brown had an idea to gain his own freedom. At 5 feet 8 inches and 200 pounds, Brown decided that he could mail himself to freedom. Two friends would help Brown with this crazy scheme: James Caesar Anthony Smith, a free Black man who sang with Brown in the choir of the First African Baptist Church, and Samuel Alexander Smith, a white shoemaker and gambler, whom Brown paid $86 to help him.[252]

A Black carpenter, John Mattaner, built a wooden box, complete with lining, air holes, and a container of water to fit Brown's size, and he was mailed to 131 Arch Street in Philadelphia.[253] After the twenty-seven-hour journey that nearly killed him, Brown arrived in Philadelphia on March 24, 1849, a free man.

What about Brown's Family?

According to Brown, he planned to get his wife and children out of enslavement. Once he became well-known from telling his escape story, his wife's captor sent a letter to Brown offering to sell him his wife and children, but Brown said no.[254] That refusal embarrassed abolitionists, who never wanted the story publicized in the first place; as Frederick Douglass lamented in 1855, "Had not Henry Box Brown and his friends attracted slaveholding attention to the manner of his escape, we might have had a thousand Box Brown's [escaping]."[255]

ESCAPING IN A BOAT

Robert Smalls was born enslaved on April 5, 1839. A captive in South Carolina, he led a life at sea as a result of his mother's request that Smalls be allowed to rent himself out to work at the harbor in Charleston, South Carolina.[256] While working in Charleston at the start of the Civil War, he earned a job on the *Planter*, a Confederate army warship. At the time, Smalls was married with two children. He wanted to purchase their freedom, but he couldn't afford the $800.[257] Smalls found another way.

When a ship was docked at a port city, like Charleston, the crew commonly would spend the night in the town and allow the enslaved crew to bring their families aboard, but then the families had to leave. On the night of May 12, 1862, the officers left the ship for a night in Charleston and allowed the families of the enslaved workers to board the ship. Smalls—who looked somewhat similar to the ship's captain and could mimic the captain's body movements— informed the other enslaved crew members that he was going to take over the ship while the Confederate officers were off the boat and then sail north to Union territory with the enslaved crew and their families onboard. Smalls was more than capable, having both the intelligence and boldness to do it.

At 3:25 a.m. on May 13, 1862, Smalls posed as the ship's captain, slyly sailed past other Confederate ships, and took the *Planter* to the Union territory in the ocean, where he surrendered the ship to Union forces. Upon arrival, Smalls, his family, and the rest of the crew and their families were free. Labeled a hero for the daring escape, Smalls was appointed a pilot in the Quartermaster's Department of the United States Navy, where he rose to the rank of captain.[258] In 1868, Smalls entered politics and was later elected to the 44th, 45th, 47th, 48th, and 49th U.S. Congresses.[259]

ESCAPING BY HIDING IN PLAIN SIGHT

William and Ellen Craft were enslaved people who lived on the same plantation in Georgia. They fell in love and their captor allowed them to marry.[260] But both understood that the horrors of enslavement could affect their marriage. It was not a guarantee that they would stay together. William came up with a plan of how the two should escape. He explained it to Ellen: "I have solved the problem of our freedom... Here is how we'll do it. You will dress up like our young master in one of his suits. You will have your hair cut like that of a young man. You are fair enough to be taken for white. Ellen, dear, you will look like a young planter elegantly dressed in a cloak and high-heeled boots."[261]

Ellen had a lot of questions. She wondered how she could pretend being a man when seen at close range or if someone approached her and she was expected to speak. She asked about what they'd do when staying overnight in a hotel. William told Ellen to cover her face as if she had a toothache so people couldn't see her face clearly and she wouldn't be expected to talk. As for staying somewhere overnight, William told Ellen that she'd have her arm in a sling so she would look injured and people would have to do things for her, like sign a guest book at a hotel.[262] With those plans, Ellen agreed, and the two prepared to escape in plain sight.

Early on, things went according to William's plan. The sling and covered face worked like a charm to avoid any suspicion. They did experience some trouble when approached by slave patrollers and in Baltimore when attempting to purchase train tickets, but William's quick thinking prevented anyone from assuming that the pair were enslaved runaways. They arrived in Philadelphia, then Boston before sailing to England in 1850, where they lived happily together and had five children.

CHAPTER 22

PASSING: ANOTHER KIND OF RESISTANCE

As a kid, while trying to figure out the complex landscape of race and skin colors, I wondered about what skin tones made Black people Black and white people white. I noticed that the skin tone of white people had some differences but not as much of a range of differences as Black people's skin. It was a subject my grade school teachers didn't really want to explore with me or my classmates (although I am not sure if they wondered about it like I did). I wondered because while my mother and I share the same skin tone, relatively speaking, my father is light skinned, his father was dark skinned, and his mother's skin tone was more like his.

Meanwhile, my mother's mother was dark skinned, but her father was light skinned, like my dad. Yet all these people both identified as and considered themselves as Black people. As a kid, I wondered why there was so much variation. Eventually, I found out that Blacks had sexual relationships with whites during enslavement and that DNA (units in the body made of chemicals that partly define a person's traits) determines the color of one's skin tone depending on the strength or weakness of traits in one's genes (the specific grouping of the chemical units that make up DNA).

THE VIOLENCE OF INTERRACIAL RELATIONS

The relations between Africans and Europeans during enslavement generally weren't pleasant. Physical and mental violence was at the root of Black and white interactions during this period, and such violence was at the root of many sexual encounters between them and even between enslaved Blacks. Captors would have sex with

their enslaved captives, often by force or some other form of violence—usually white men forcing Black women to have sex.

Children born of those relations were usually enslaved. If those
children were girls, they too were likely to have to provide sexual
pleasure to their white captors. To be clear, white women engaged
in forced sexual relations in many forms with Black men as well.

What Is the "One Drop Rule"?

This is a belief that any person who has "one drop" of African blood
is actually Black. In other words, if a white person is found to have
any African ancestry due to interracial sexual relations during
enslavement, that person is legally categorized as Black. Who was
Black in someone's ancestry would determine how "Black" a person
was. For example, if a person had one white parent and one Black
parent, that person was a mulatto or one-half Black; if a person had
three white grandparents and one Black grandparent, that person
was labeled a quadroon or one-quarter Black; and so on.

WHAT IS PASSING?

Passing is when a person is regarded as or believed to be a member
of a certain group—in this case a racial group—but is not a member
of that group. The same idea can apply to religious groups or social
class groups, but more often than not, the term "passing" is used to
describe individuals who seem to belong to a racial group they are
not truly a member of.

Hypothetically speaking, a child with a white dad and biracial
mom could appear to be a white person, so much so that others
may believe that the child has no African ancestry. That person,
whether male or female, might have access to benefits that other
enslaved Black people did not have. Even though enslaved people
like this were considered Black on a plantation where their ancestry
was known, off the plantation was another story. Their ability to pass

because of their skin tone might offer benefits, such as being able to learn how to read and write. For enslaved people in this situation, taking advantage of the assumption that a light-skinned person was white became a way to escape enslavement and to live life as a white person to maintain their freedom.

For example, an Alabama man who was the captor of an escaped enslaved woman named Fanny wrote in an advertisement in the June 14, 1845, edition of the *Alabama Beacon* to retrieve her that "she is as white as most white women, with straight light hair, and blue eyes, and can pass herself for a white woman."[263] Fanny's ability to read and write certainly helped her ability to pass as white. Although some scholars argue that racial passing began regularly in the mid- to late nineteenth century, reaching its peak in the early twentieth century and then subsiding by the 1930s, the example of Fanny shows passing has a longer and more extensive early history.[264]

Whiteness—although it's a made-up category with no scientific standing—became a real thing with freedom and benefits attached to it, while Blackness had attached to it inferiority and evil that were markers of shame and worthlessness. While the meaning of Black or Blackness isn't the same as it was in antebellum America, it still doesn't measure up to whiteness in twenty-first century America.

THE RATIONALE FOR PASSING

Many have accused those who passed as white as guilty of being ashamed of who they are. But as mentioned earlier, Blackness has attached to it the idea of inferiority, whether it has to do with beauty, intelligence, creativity, cleverness, accomplishment, and so on. This was a result of the slavocracy (society ruled by enslavers) designed to take advantage of Black people for the desires of their captors, including profit and pleasure.

No one wishes to be captured, and if there is an opportunity for escape—including acting like a white person because people think you're a white person—one takes it. One could argue that it was better to be like Ellen Craft, who was able to use her light skin tone to escape to freedom, than to live life as a white person. (See "Great Escapes during the Antebellum" on page 92 for more on Ellen Craft.) But when you live in a society where whiteness is the key to freedom, social position, and safety, it makes sense to pass versus remaining enslaved.

It's easy to blame Black people who did this as self-hating or accepting their "whiteness" and "Blackness" as equal parts of their identity. But they were born to an anti-Black world, a world where being Black brought shame and violence because of the country that made that law. Rather than question Black people who used passing for their survival, we should question the society and "leaders" that forced the act of passing upon them.

CHAPTER 23

THE DISASTERS OF CHIRIQUÍ AND ÎLE À VACHE

In June 2019, when President Donald Trump instructed four American women of color—who happened to be serving in Congress[265]—via tweet to "go back" to the countries they came from, he tapped into a painful history.[266] (These women were Rashida Tlaib from Michigan, Ilhan Omar from Minnesota, Ayanna Pressley from Massachusetts, and Alexandria Ocasio-Cortez from New York.) When Black people are specifically the target of that negative command—to "go back"—which is often said to them because they've challenged white supremacy or systemic racism in some way, the words "to Africa" are added.

That specific phrase, "go back to Africa," is rooted in white America's desire to bleach away the bloodstains of its original sin: enslavement.[267] An early example of it is found in the work of the American Colonization Society, or ACS, an organization that stood for the complete opposite of resistance and rebellion for Africans. The ACS was more of the same—ordering the African where to go.

THE AMERICAN COLONIZATION SOCIETY

The ACS, born in Congress, was a white-male originated and led organization started in 1816 with the purpose of resettling free Black people (who were either emancipated or born free) in Africa—not in the territory of their ancestry, just somewhere in Africa. This method alone was disrespectful and showed a lack of knowledge of African humanity. The belief was the only way African people could be tolerated in the United States was as enslaved people; non-enslaved Black people couldn't fit into white society.

They received the support of people in the government and the financial support of philanthropists (people who generously donate money to social causes), who provided funding to purchase the freedom of enslaved Africans and their descendants, cover the cost of their travel, and support their adjustment to West Africa. One supporter was President James Monroe, after whom the capital of Liberia (Monrovia) is named; Liberia was a colony of the United States set up in West Africa specifically as a place for free Blacks to live. In 1822, the group began sending freed Blacks to Liberia, and thousands of Blacks would eventually settle there.

Some scholars believe that the ACS genuinely wished to abolish slavery and resettle Blacks for their own well-being; but others see the effort as a politically quick way to deal with a growing number of freed Blacks in the upper South.[268] The reality is that the ACS was rooted in the idea that recolonizing (creating a new settlement for) Africans would end the pollution of America's morals (ideas of what behavior is right) by Blacks as well as grow the economic opportunities for whites.[269] For members of the ACS, African recolonization (creating a new colony) was the only way to go. Decades later, President Abraham Lincoln thought along similar lines.

A MEETING OF THE MINDS

During his first year as president in 1861, Lincoln was obsessed with persuading free Blacks to lead a mass departure of African Americans out of the United States, enabling the country to wash away the original sin of slavery without its citizens having to live alongside those the country had enslaved.[270] He just had to persuade influential Black people to lead this mass departure. To that end, on August 14, 1862, Lincoln met with a group of Black leaders to discuss the matter: "Edward M. Thomas, messenger to the House of Representatives and a respected cultural leader in Washington's Black community; John F. Cook Jr., a local school leader who had studied at Oberlin College; John T. Costin, who, like Thomas and Cook, was a Freemason; Cornelius Clark, a member of the influential Social,

Civil, and Statistical Association in Washington (Cook and Thomas also were members); and Benjamin M. McCoy, a teacher and leader in the Asbury Methodist Episcopal Church in Washington."[271]

In advising them that the best way for Blacks to help the Union effort was to leave,[272] the president started the conversation as follows:

You and we are different races.... We have between us a broader difference than exists between almost any other two races. Your race suffers very greatly, many of them, by living among us, while ours suffers from your presence. In a word, we suffer on each side. If this is admitted, it affords a reason at least why we should be separated.... If intelligent colored men, such as are before me, would move in this matter, much might be accomplished. It is exceedingly important that we have men at the beginning capable of thinking as white men, and not those who have been systematically oppressed.[273]

The reaction from the group of leaders Lincoln spoke with differed from the feeling of the wider Black community. While the Black leaders seemed open to Lincoln's agenda, that community met Lincoln's words with outrage and despair. They were also angered that this group of leaders thought they represented anyone in the Black community.[274] Nevertheless, Lincoln continued with his plan. He had multiple sites in mind for recolonization, including Panama and Haiti.

In April 1862, Congress passed the District of Columbia Emancipation Act, which provided payment on emancipation to the capital's approximately three thousand enslaved Blacks. That summer, Congress added an additional $500,000 for colonization purposes, creating a fund of $600,000 for the president to use for recolonization.[275] Lincoln just had to seal the deal.

THE DISASTER OF CHIRIQUÍ

The plan for Panama was led by Ambrose Thompson, a white man, who claimed to have thousands of acres of land in the Chiriquí province to settle free Blacks there. Lincoln was a fan of the plan as early as spring 1861, seeing it as the best destination for government-sponsored colonization.[276] Even with doubt among the Black community, racism and overcrowding persuaded some to attempt the move to Chiriquí.

On August 16, 1862, Lincoln accepted an offer from Kansas Senator Samuel C. Pomeroy to organize Black immigration (the act of entering a land called Linconia and settling there) parties to Central America, and on September 11, he authorized Caleb Smith, Lincoln's Secretary of the Interior, to sign an agreement with Thompson giving money to develop the coal mines there. On September 24, however, two days after issuing the preliminary Emancipation Proclamation, Lincoln stopped Pomeroy's operation.[277]

The project failed because of uncertainty about the ownership of the land, a lack of support from Central American governments, and the discovery that the coal that was supposed to support the territory and make the U.S. money was worthless. Left behind were the hundreds of Black people, who had sold their homes, furniture, and possessions to live in Panama, now without a place to live in the United States.

THE DISASTER OF ÎLE À VACHE

The plan for Haiti was designed by Bernard Kock, a white man, who had secured a lease of an island off the coast of Haiti called Île à Vache, where he planned to settle Black people. Although Haiti was a source of inspiration and pride for Black people, word reached U.S. Black people that immigrants to Haiti were often treated shabbily by locals and that the Haitian government did far less than promised to help them.[278]

On April 14, 1863, with the backing of both Lincoln and the Haitian government, a ship carrying four hundred fifty-three formerly enslaved people departed from Virginia to Haiti, but Kock proved to be an incapable leader, and the Haitian colony failed miserably.[279] The island was underprepared for the new arrivals, disease was widespread, the island was undersupplied, and Kock thought of himself as having complete power.[280] Kock fled the island under threat of revolt. Of the initial four hundred fifty-three named colonists, two hundred ninety-two remained on Île à Vache, an additional seventy-three fled to the Haitian mainland, and the rest died from disease and starvation.[281]

CHAPTER 24

THE BATTLE OF PINE SWAMP AT TIMBUCTOO

When learning about Black history as a kid, I associated it with the South and major U.S. cities. That's because those were typically the settings of the stories included in the Black history we learned. I was born and raised in New Jersey—southern New Jersey (South Jersey is what we call it) to be specific—and I always wondered if Black history happened here. As I grew older, I realized that wherever Black people were, (Black) history was made.

New Jersey may not be the first place one thinks of for Black history, but Black history happened in my home state, including in areas I am familiar with. For example, Harriet Tubman frequented South Jersey because of the free Black settlements there that served as stops on the Underground Railroad. (See "Harriet Tubman: The Greatest American Who Ever Was" on page 110 for more on Harriet Tubman.) She also spent time in Cape May, New Jersey, on the coast, between 1849 and 1852, working as a servant in hotels to earn money for her rescue attempts in the South.[282]

FREE BLACK SETTLEMENTS

Free Black settlements in New Jersey arose in part because of Quaker communities, which served as "conductors" and created safe houses for Blacks escaping enslavement along the southwestern portion of the state. Unlike North Jersey, South Jersey was a haven for enslaved persons escaping captivity. Between 1840 and 1860, the population of free Black people in South Jersey grew from 5,524 people to 9,853, a growth of 78 percent versus 13 percent growth in North Jersey at that time.[283]

Recently emancipated Blacks started communities near Quaker areas with the help of Quakers, who provided Black people with legal protections. For the town Timbuctoo, local Quakers sold land to African Americans at below-market-rate prices.[284] Also, Black people found work in Quaker towns. Black people worked with Quakers to secure the safety and freedom of enslaved escapees along sections of the Underground Railroad.

Black residents formed close communities in towns, living in homes near one another. This was true for Timbuctoo, whose clustered housing arrangements very likely offered not only a community spirit but also protection from outside harmful forces.[285]

Timbuctoo existed during enslavement in southern New Jersey, specifically during the Fugitive Slave Act of 1853. This law allowed slave hunters to venture into Northern states to recapture escaped enslaved people. Community members depended on one another for protection[286] because hunters coming north to recapture formerly enslaved persons would also seize free Black people.

The Original Timbuktu

Timbuctoo in New Jersey wasn't the first town with that name. The townspeople took the name from Timbuktu, the famed city of the Mali empire. Timbuktu, founded at the end of the fifth century CE, was the intellectual heart of the empire and home to the University of Sankore—the education center of West Africa. The university featured top professors, and students from all over the Muslim world came to Timbuktu to study many subjects, including literacy, law, and medicine—surgery, in particular. The city also prospered economically until the fall of the empire.

THE BATTLE OF PINE SWAMP

In December 1860, a group of hunters of enslaved persons attempted to recapture Perry Simmons, who had been enslaved but

RESISTANCE STORIES *from* BLACK HISTORY *for* KIDS

had escaped captivity and had been free for ten years. He and his family were staying in a farmhouse on Pine Swamp Road, owned by Allen Fenimore. The slave catchers included a U.S. marshal[287]—who was a well-known captor of formerly enslaved persons and who belonged to the U.S. Marshal's Office whose functions included organizing fugitive operations—six to eight men from Camden, New Jersey, and Philadelphia, and a Black informant who used to live in Timbuctoo. Just as there were Blacks who were traitors (those who betray friends) who betrayed the rebellions of the enslaved, there were those who betrayed those who had escaped captivity.

The caravan of captors reached Simmons's residence around midnight and knocked on the door, saying they had a warrant for Simmons's arrest for stealing chickens. Alarmed by the notification, Simmons gathered his family and retreated to the attic, where he was armed and ready for the worst. Tired of waiting for Simmons to open the door, the men broke it down, entered the home, and called for Simmons to surrender, but he did not. The well-known captor attempted to enter the attic to retrieve Simmons and his family, but he quickly changed his mind when the barrel of Simmons's gun greeted him as he reached the attic opening. The men decided to camp out at the home and wait out Simmons.

They started a fire and got cozy. All the while, the people in the attic occasionally yelled "kidnappers" or "murderers" loud enough for anyone outside to hear. At 6:30 a.m., Fenimore's son, who worked for Simmons, heard the family yell "kidnappers." Once he saw the house and the carriages, he went to Timbuctoo and alerted the town. The townspeople quickly armed themselves and marched to the farmhouse.

The *New Jersey Mirror*, the local paper for Burlington County, said the residents "turned out en masse, and armed themselves with every conceivable weapon, were soon on a 'quick march' for the field of strife, yelling and screaming at the top of their voices."[288] When the captors heard what the paper called the "Timbuctoo Warriors," they quickly left the farmhouse.

Certainly, the Black informant got away as soon as he could. If he was a spy who tipped off those captors about Simmons, for a price, he would have betrayed others like Simmons living in Timbuctoo. Those warriors of Timbuctoo would have been enraged upon seeing his face.

As for Simmons and his family, they probably left the area. While Simmons had lived free for ten years, he could have reasonably assumed those men would return, with more men. It was possible that the town of roughly one hundred twenty-five people[289] would not have been able to save Simmons, or themselves, if there were a next time.

BY THE NUMBERS: FREE BLACKS IN THE UNITED STATES*

488,070

Free Blacks living in the United States by 1860

83,492

Free Blacks living in Maryland by 1860—the largest population in the U.S.

52.6%

Free Blacks in the South who were female in 1860

226,152

Free Blacks in the North in 1860

261,918

Free Blacks living in the South by 1860

18%

Free Blacks living in Delaware—the largest percentage in the Union

15

Different states where free Black people lived

20%

Free Blacks over the age of 40

7.5%

Free Blacks who owned slaves by 1830

*   Gates, "Slavery, by the Numbers."
    Wolfe, "Slavery by the Numbers (Redux)."

CHAPTER 25

HARRIET TUBMAN: THE GREATEST AMERICAN WHO EVER WAS

In my humble opinion, Harriet Tubman was the greatest American who ever lived. Many people know of her adventures as leader of the Underground Railroad. But I am unsure if people truly appreciate the danger of leading enslaved African peoples to freedom and the courage it took to repeatedly return to the South to free more of them. I am sure her courage to lead Black people to freedom was a reason for the push early in the twenty-first century to add her image to the $20 bill. I believe that many descendants of Africans throughout U.S. history could replace any of the presidents already pictured on our currency.

However, I feel that this gesture is a slap in the face of Tubman and her legacy. Her work involved liberating the very people exchanged for the very currency the government wanted to post her picture on. Tubman's legacy is one of courage, strength, determination, and faith. It's the kind of legacy that would have nothing to do with the ideas of capitalism (the U.S. economic system based on competing to make money for goods and services), ideas that Tubman didn't support. She put people before profit and the lives of others above her own. Our country is better for her having lived as a rebel and resister.

SHE RESISTED DEATH

Harriet Tubman was born Araminta "Minty" Ross in 1822 to Ben Ross and Harriet Green. As her captor moved to a new location in Maryland, Araminta, her siblings, and her mother were moved with the captor and ten miles away from Ben Ross.[290] As a child, Araminta was rented out for work by her captor; she was the first of his captives to be hired out. Some of the farmers she worked for were cruel and negligent, and she bore the scars of their whippings for the rest of her life.[291] She even survived measles as a child, which can cause pneumonia and death.

Between the ages of twelve and fourteen, Araminta and another enslaved person were sent to the store to pick up a few items and there they saw an enslaved Black trying to escape but his overseer caught him. When asked to help tie him up, Araminta refused. Because of her refusal, she was mistakenly hit on the head with a 2-pound weight that was meant for the fleeing Black. The impact broke Araminta's skull. Just as the measles was life threatening, so was her head trauma. Even so, Araminta was forced to continue to work.[292] Her recovery was considered a miracle.

Human Capital

Because enslaved African people were considered property and not people, they were used like credit to get loans to start a business or purchase property. They were also exchanged or sold by their captors to get out of debt, which is what happened with Araminta's family. Her sisters were sold to keep their captor out of debt. In addition, enslaved people were given as gifts by wealthier captors.

SHE RESISTED HER PLIGHT

Araminta suffered from the cruel nature of enslavement, not just physically but emotionally. Enslavement tore her family apart, as her captor sold members of her family to other captors. Thankfully, her father was freed, but her remaining siblings were in danger of being sold. At this time, she was married to John Tubman and she adopted her mother's name (Harriet) as her own. She was allowed to keep some of her earnings, and when she realized that she could be sold next because of another illness she had, she chose to flee.[293]

Her first attempt involved fleeing with her brothers, but they had a change of heart and didn't care that Tubman wanted to keep going.[294] She returned with her brothers and faced punishment for fleeing, but she didn't remain for long. On October 3, 1849, Tubman left the only home she had ever known and resolved never to be enslaved again. Although she left her family behind when she escaped, she didn't leave them behind for long. In 1850, she returned to rescue her niece and her niece's two children.[295] A year or so later, she went back to rescue her youngest brother and several other individuals along the way.

SHE RESISTED HEARTBREAK

In the fall of 1851, Tubman returned to her home to rescue her husband, only to find out that he had moved on with his life and had remarried a free woman[296] with whom he had no worries about their children being enslaved. This mattered because while married to John, she had no children. One reason was out of fear of losing her children since she was enslaved at the time of her marriage. So, Tubman moved on. Scholar Erica Armstrong Dunbar described the situation:

She planned to approach the new couple's cabin and [according to Harriet] "go right in and make all the trouble she could." But a cooler head prevailed. Harriet realized that she could not risk her own safety with a physical confrontation that would certainly bring unwanted attention and possibly capture. She was upset but wasn't stupid. "If he could do without her, she could do without him," Harriet realized. She let John Tubman go.[297]

A Moses for Her People

The story of Moses's rescue of the ancient Israelites is important in both the Jewish and Christian religions. Moses, at the call (and

RESISTANCE STORIES *from* BLACK HISTORY *for* KIDS

with the help) of God, brought the Israelites from enslavement to freedom. This story inspired enslaved Blacks to have faith in Jesus Christ, whom Christians believe to be the son of God. As a conductor on the Underground Railroad, Harriet Tubman ushered Blacks from enslavement to freedom—as Moses did with his people—with the help of Jesus, as she said.[298] For that reason, Tubman was given the nickname "Moses" by abolitionist William Lloyd Garrison.

SHE CONTINUED TO RESIST

After moving on from her husband, Tubman continued to venture back into enslaved territories to free African people throughout the south. In the thirteen trips back, she saved about seventy people, including friends, relatives, and even her parents—saving her father from possible arrest for helping enslaved Blacks run away.[299] To support these trips, she worked various jobs, including working as a hotel cook in Cape May, New Jersey, a South Jersey shore town where she lived for a time in an established Black community.[300]

Tubman secured a home for her family in both Albany, New York, and later Canada, and offered support for and strategized with abolitionists John Brown and Frederick Douglass, conducting her last rescue mission in 1860. After that, Tubman served as a scout, spy, and leader of Black Union troops against rebel Confederate forces, liberating seven hundred enslaved Blacks in the process. All these accomplishments happened by the time Tubman reached her early forties. She devoted the rest of her life to her family, Black people, women's suffrage (right to vote), and telling her story... a story like no other.

CHAPTER 26

THE REAL INDEPENDENCE DAY

The Fourth of July in the United States is known as Independence Day—the day in 1776 that the Declaration of Independence was signed. I learned this in school, as you probably did. But the truth is that all people weren't made independent with the document. African people weren't made free. If I had been alive in the thirteen colonies on July 4, 1776, I—most likely—would have been enslaved. Therefore, I don't celebrate the day.

It doesn't make sense when declaring independence that independence was not for all. When you look at the Declaration of Independence, its words don't suggest anything other than freedom for all. Yet there is always a story behind the story. In the case of the Declaration of Independence, the story behind the story offers information on what the words actually mean.

DRAFTING THE DECLARATION

Some of the most famous words of the Declaration of Independence are "all men are created equal." However, those weren't the original words. The first draft of the Declaration specifically states: "All men are born equally free and independent and have certain inherent natural rights of which they cannot, by any compact, deprive or divest their posterity; among which are the enjoyment of life, liberty, with the means of acquiring and possessing property, and pursuing and obtaining happiness and safety."[301]

These exact words are not part of the final Declaration of Independence, because these words are pure and inclusive, how the language should be. But some Virginia delegates believed that this language encouraged enslaved Blacks to rebel and supported the abolition of enslavement altogether.[302] The original language was edited numerous times to reflect enslavement as a necessity of the new country.

Thomas Jefferson reworked the original draft so it allowed enslavement and did not equate white men with Black people. To do so, he specifically replaced "born" with "created" and "property" with "the pursuit of happiness."[303] Those simple changes made the language less clear so the colonists could both declare freedom from England and own Blacks without being criticized for their hypocrisy (behaving in a way that is the opposite of what one claims to believe).

The Declaration of Independence was not a document that included Black people, let alone other nonwhite men. The same is true for the Constitution. Liberty and freedom applied only to white men. Therefore, July 4, 1776, is an "Independence Day" only for white men (white, Anglo-Saxon, Protestant landowners, to be exact), and independence for some is not independence for all. Of July 4, Frederick Douglass said:

What, to the American slave, is your 4th of July? I answer; a day that reveals to him, more than all other days in the year, the gross injustice and cruelty to which he is the constant victim. To him, your celebration is a sham; your boasted liberty, an unholy license; your national greatness, swelling vanity; your sounds of rejoicing are empty and heartless; your denunciation of tyrants, brass fronted impudence; your shouts of liberty and equality, hollow mockery; your prayers and hymns, your sermons and thanksgivings, with all your religious parade and solemnity, are, to Him, mere bombast, fraud, deception, impiety, and hypocrisy—a thin veil to cover up crimes which would disgrace a nation of savages.[304]

Douglass was saying that while the Fourth of July represented freedom for white men, it didn't for Black people. American independence was rooted in maintaining enslavement, so why should Black people celebrate it?

THE GENERAL STRIKE AND JUNETEENTH

The Civil War, fought from 1861 to 1865, was a war between Northern states (Union states or the United States of America) and Southern states that had separated from the United States (Confederate states or the Confederate States of America). The Civil War, not the American Revolution, was a war for the independence of all peoples in the United States.

African people fought in the American Revolution, but they fought on both sides of the war, seeking a guarantee of freedom wherever they could find it. (See "The Birth of a Nation" on page 33 for more about the roots of the Revolutionary War.) However, during the Civil War, the sides were clear. Though it was—as scholar and activist W. E. B. DuBois said—a white man's war to preserve the Union, it indeed turned into a war for Black liberation. And Black people fought on the side of their own liberation.[305] DuBois described this:

As soon, however, as it became clear that the Union armies would not or could not return fugitive slaves, and that the masters with all their fume and fury were uncertain of victory, the slave entered upon a general strike against slavery by the same methods that he had used during the period of the fugitive slave; he ran away to the first place of safety and offered his services to the Federal Army.[306]

That fight immediately began with what DuBois called a general strike, during which Blacks all over the South left plantations and sought refuge with the Northern army when that army arrived in Southern territory, often joining the Northern army against the South. This is how DuBois described the strike: "This was not merely the desire to stop work. It was a strike on a wide basis against the conditions of work. It was a general strike that involved directly in the end perhaps a half million people. They wanted to stop the economy of the plantation system, and to do that they left the plantations."[307]

Along with the North's recognition of its dependence on Black people to win the war came the Emancipation Proclamation, an executive order by President Abraham Lincoln on January 1, 1863,

RESISTANCE STORIES *from* BLACK HISTORY *for* KIDS

that freed all enslaved Blacks in Confederate states. But that did not end enslavement; the Thirteenth Amendment did, ratified on January 31, 1865.

But word of the Confederate surrender and passage of the Thirteenth Amendment didn't reach all the South until June 19, 1865, when Union troops arrived in Galveston, Texas, to announce that all enslaved people were free upon the surrender of the last Confederate stronghold[308] via General Order Number 3. It states: "The people of Texas are informed that in accordance with a Proclamation from the Executive of the United States, all slaves are free. This involves an absolute equality of rights and rights of property between former masters and slaves, and the connection heretofore existing between them becomes that between employer and hired laborer."[309]

The Start of Juneteenth

An article in the *Progressive* magazine describes the holiday's start: "Before Juneteenth became Juneteenth, it was first celebrated in 1866, in Texas, as Emancipation Day. Other states had their own Emancipation Days, but importantly, outside of Texas, Emancipation Day took place on January 1, rather than in June, to match with the anniversary of the Emancipation Proclamation. While Galveston was the last Confederate territory where enslavement was declared dead, it was still allowed in a handful of states—Delaware and Kentucky, for example—until the passage of the Thirteenth Amendment in December 1865."[310]

WHAT IS JUNETEENTH?

"Juneteenth" is a combination of words "June" and "nineteenth." Juneteenth is also known as Freedom Day or Emancipation Day. The Thirteen Amendment guaranteed freedom for all people regardless of their race immediately while in and upon arrival to the United

States. That document created a freer society, but like the Declaration, it was not perfect—the clause that allows enslavement for those in prison has fueled the mass incarceration (imprisonment) of Black people and the corporate use (over four thousand one hundred businesses participate) of prison labor.[311]

How Was Juneteenth Originally Celebrated?

A *Progressive* magazine article describes Juneteenth celebrations: "Early Juneteenth celebrations looked like community gatherings: sports were played, cookouts were held, and Black folks prayed, danced, and lit fireworks. But at their core, these events were an opportunity for both community empowerment and for families broken up by enslavement to reconnect. Juneteenth gatherings customarily feature red foods—such as strawberry pie, barbecue, watermelon, hot sauce, red rice, red velvet cake, red drink, and red sausages—to symbolize toughness, resistance, and joy."[312]

Juneteenth offers Americans the best opportunity to celebrate the independence of all peoples in the United States. In 2021, President Joe Biden signed a law making Juneteenth a federal holiday. It raises the question, however: Will we celebrate an actual recognition of independence or the anniversary of a white settler colonial project? The truth is that you really cannot celebrate both. My suggestion is to celebrate Juneteenth. What about July 4th? Use that day as an opportunity to point people to Juneteenth and use what you have learned here to provide them the reasons why.

CHAPTER 27

GIVING CREDIT WHERE CREDIT IS DUE

No one becomes successful on their own. Along one's journey to success, individuals or groups provide help and support. When those people come along and provide that all-important help and support, it is important to acknowledge them and give them the credit they deserve. Sometimes, these folks prefer to be in the background, and that's OK. But they still deserve recognition for their contributions to the success of another.

I can remember failing to be acknowledged for my role in the success of someone else—whether it had to do with my role in a class project or my role in helping someone prepare for a test, it didn't feel good not to be acknowledged. Sadly, American history has numerous examples of Black people failing to be acknowledged for their contributions to the success of others, specifically white people.

FAILING TO BE ACKNOWLEDGED

Some examples of failing to get acknowledgment are recent. In 2021, for example, a white person got credit for and was invited to appear on TV on the *Tonight Show* to perform a number of popular TikTok dances that had been created by Black dancers.[313] That event helped cause Black artists to go on strike against TikTok. The artists and Black TikTok users were fed up and frustrated with the way Black creativity on apps like TikTok is constantly stolen and replicated to profit others.[314] This history of taking credit from creative Black people dates to the time of enslavement.

This happened to an enslaved person, Nearest Green. He taught Jack Daniels how to make whiskey, a type of alcohol. Starting in the 1850s and continuing after the Civil War, Green oversaw an important part of making[315] the whiskey while working for Daniels.[316] (Distillation is the process of making whiskey by separating alcoholic liquids from fermented items, usually foods items transformed into alcoholic materials.) Jack Daniels's brand of whiskey became one of the more popular and successful whiskeys in the world. Green is just one example of not getting proper credit. Although we may not consider the creation of an alcoholic beverage nearly as important as the creation of the telephone or the lightbulb, the man behind them, a Black man, wasn't recognized for his contribution to those two inventions.

BLACK INVENTOR LEWIS LATIMER

Lewis Latimer is the man behind the telephone and the lightbulb. Alexander Graham Bell approached him in 1876 to prepare the precise blueprints and to assist in the detailed descriptions needed to obtain the patent (an official document that gives ownership to an invention) for his remarkable invention, the telephone.[317]

It is true that Bell invented the telephone, but without Latimer's contribution to the patent and the plans and directions for building the device, the telephone may never have been built. Latimer also worked with Thomas Edison to help improve Edison's electric lamp. Before joining Edison, in the 1880s Latimer had patented a procedure for manufacturing an improved part for the lamp that conducts the electricity; he also devised an improved and standard lamp base.[318]

He was America's pioneer in lighting city streets and large buildings with the electric lamp, and his publication *Incandescent Lighting: A Practical Description of the Edison System* was a standard text in the field.[319] Sadly, Latimer didn't receive as much credit as Bell or Edison for his contributions to their success. Nevertheless, without his work, it may have taken longer to create these items that we rely on so much today. The next time you get on your cell phone or turn on a light, be sure to thank Latimer.

Other Inventions by Black Inventors

Some inventions we cannot live without came from Black inventors. They include the following:

- Traffic light (Garrett Morgan)
- Refrigerated truck (Frederick McKinley Jones)
- Electric microphone (James E. West)
- Shoe-molding machine (Jan Earnst Matzeliger)
- Home security system (Mary Van Brittan Brown)
- Railroad car automating system (Andrew Jackson Beard)
- Sugar evaporator (Norbert Rillieux)
- Steamboat propeller (Benjamin Montgomery)
- Central heating furnace (Alice H. Parker)
- Ironing board (Elijah McCoy)
- Peanut products, including cooking oil, milk, and soap (George Washington Carver)
- Super Soaker water gun (Lonnie Johnson)
- Almanac with astronomical calculations (Benjamin Banneker)
- Improved ironing board (Sarah Boone)
- Automatic elevator doors (Alexander Miles)

CHAPTER 28

THE ORIGIN AND PURPOSE OF BLACK HISTORY MONTH

In February 1992, my grade-school principal elected my second-grade class to participate in a Black History Month celebration during which we would recite speeches by famous African Americans. I was given parts of two speeches: a speech by Nobel Peace Prize–winning diplomat Ralph Bunche and another by minister and civil rights leader Martin Luther King Jr. I recited those speeches twice. The first time was at a school assembly. The second was at a Black History Month celebration at my school held on a Saturday evening.

During the second event when it was my turn to recite my portion of King's "I Have a Dream" speech, you could hear a pin drop. I realized in that moment, at eight years old, that what I was about to say was very important. Those in the audience didn't come to hear me; rather, they came to hear the words of King. It was the first time I realized that Black History Month was a big deal. Sadly, as I grew older, the significance of Black History Month lessened to me. This wasn't because Black history wasn't important, but because it wasn't treated by those teaching it with the importance it deserved.

Who Is Ralph Bunche?

Ralph Bunche (1903–1971) was a political scientist (someone who analyzes politics and the government) who taught at both Howard and Harvard universities and was an activist during the civil rights movement. In addition, he was a famous diplomat (someone who specializes in interactions between nations) who won the Nobel Peace Prize for helping negotiate a peace agreement in the Middle East in 1949.

WHAT BLACK HISTORY MONTH HAS BECOME

Whether intentional or not, kids are often taught that Black history began with the enslavement of African people and concluded with King's "I Have a Dream" speech. Of course, the occasional Black athlete, politician, and entertainer are highlighted during the month for good measure. In the 1990s, for example, teachers would put up posters of TV celebrities, athletes, and government folks like Oprah Winfrey, Michael Jordan, and Colin Powell. Today, it's Beyoncé, LeBron James, and Barack Obama. Focusing only on a few people who made history makes sense, considering that Black History Month is celebrated in February, the shortest month of the year.

That's the running joke—that the United States is so racist that Black people received the shortest month to celebrate our accomplishments and our history. Schools put up the same Black history posters each February, only to take them down immediately on March 1. That extra day during leap year in February seems like just a glitch in the matrix. Assigning Black History Month to February and learning only about "Black stuff"—which usually means teaching enslavement—can seem like a racist conspiracy. But this wasn't the original idea behind the celebration.

WHAT BLACK HISTORY MONTH WAS MEANT TO BE

In 1926, historian Carter G. Woodson created Negro History Week, which later became Black History Month. This came out of his goal to educate Black children and Black people overall by way of his organization, the Association for the Study of Negro Life and History (ASNLH). He wanted to publicize the work of ASNLH across the nation and get more people to invest in the organization.[320]

But his main purpose was to focus on the achievements of Black people to get educators to add this information to coursework that covered Black culture and history.[321] The weeklong celebration was an opportunity for young people, Black children specifically, to review all the lessons and history they learned about Black people throughout the year.

The reason why February is Black History Month is that Woodson chose to celebrate Negro History Week during the week of Frederick Douglass's (February 14) and Abraham Lincoln's (February 12) birthdays. If the birthdays happened to fall on different weeks, the week of Douglass's birthday was the week for the event.

What Is Critical Race Theory?

Critical race theory is an academic idea that says throughout American history, patterns of racism are found in American law and other institutions in society, for example, banking, education, and criminal justice. It also states that the impact of enslavement and segregation continues to create an uneven playing field for Black people and other people of color.

It's hard to say exactly what Woodson would think about what occurs during Black History Month today. Most likely he would hate the complaints that Black History Month celebrations are the same thing as critical race theory. These complaints are an attempt to prevent the telling of Black history to avoid making white people feel uncomfortable.[322]

According to what Woodson said previously, he wouldn't agree with some of the ways Black History Month is presented to students: "It is evident from the numerous calls for orators during Negro History Week that schools and their administrators do not take the study of the Negro seriously enough to use Negro History Month as a short period for demonstrating what the students have learned in their study of the Negro during the whole school year."[323]

It can be nice when speakers come to classes to give speeches for Black History Month. But in many schools, these speeches are part of a regularly scheduled program that covers Black history during February and at no other time. If it's like that at your school, just know that's not what Woodson intended. Sadly, Woodson isn't here to keep schools and their administrators in check. Once you finish this book, maybe you can.

CHAPTER 29

BLACK FREEDOM, WHITE ANGER, AND A RED SUMMER

According to school districts around the country, the history of the United States is so vast, it cannot all be covered in one year of high school; it's covered in two. These courses were favorites of mine, but I always felt there was more history to learn. Once I got to college, I realized I was right. And as a teacher who has taught both history courses, I've had the chance to teach my students the history I wasn't taught, taking a deeper look into the Reconstruction era, the formation of the Jim Crow South, and the way Black people attempted to defend themselves.

RECONSTRUCTION IN THE UNITED STATES

The Reconstruction era is the time immediately after the Civil War (1865–1877) when the U.S. government reunited Southern states with the rest of the country while attempting to provide Black people with freedoms and citizenship rights. Major laws were passed at this time, including the Thirteenth Amendment, which ended enslavement (except for people in prison); the Fourteenth Amendment, which made formerly enslaved persons American citizens with equal protection under the law; and the Fifteenth Amendment, which gave all American male citizens the right to vote. Women weren't given the right to vote until the passage of the Nineteenth Amendment in 1920.

Reconstruction-era laws also allowed Black people to become state representatives and congressmen. Hiram Revels, who had organized two Black Army regiments during the Civil War, became the first Black person to serve in either house of Congress (he was a

Republican member of the U.S. Senate representing Mississippi). In total, sixteen Black men served in Congress, over six hundred were elected to state legislatures, and hundreds more held local offices—mostly throughout Southern states. Unfortunately, Black representation as well as the protection of the rights of Black people came to an end with an agreement among members of Congress known as the Compromise of 1877.[324]

The Compromise of 1877

The Compromise of 1877 came about after the presidential election of 1876. Although Democrats declared their candidate, Samuel B. Tilden, the winner, Republicans accused them of scaring away Black voters from voting to help their candidate win. After numerous discussions, Democrats agreed to concede, or grant the election win, to the Republican candidate, Rutherford B. Hayes. This was in exchange for removing U.S. troops sent to protect the rights of Black people in the Southern (formerly Confederate) states, leading to the end of the Reconstruction era.

BLACK CODES AND THE DAWN OF THE JIM CROW SOUTH

Once U.S. troops left the South, Southern states no longer acknowledged laws passed during Reconstruction and enforced laws they created immediately after the end of enslavement. Those laws were called Black Codes, a series of laws that both limited the freedom of Black people and forced them to remain as a group of cheap laborers, much like enslaved people. The only difference was that Black people were paid a small amount of money.

Examples of Black Codes include laws stating that Black people had to have a job or they would be sent to prison, where, according to the Thirteenth Amendment, they could be enslaved. Also, the

Black Codes declared that Black people could work only as servants or farmers. Other Black Codes prevented Black people from voting in elections.

States that passed laws like these to segregate, dominate, discriminate against, and scare Black people were part of the Jim Crow South. This area was made up of the former Confederate states, for example, Georgia, Mississippi, Alabama, South Carolina, and so on. These laws came from the U.S. Supreme Court's 1896 decision Plessy v. Ferguson. The court's decision legalized "separate but equal" facilities. The laws were named Jim Crow after a racist character named Jumpin' Jim Crow, a stereotypical portrayal of an enslaved African American played by white actors in performances called minstrel shows.

THE GREAT MIGRATION AND THE RED SUMMER

Jim Crow laws not only restricted the rights of Black people but also allowed white people to get away with being violent toward Black people. A common form of violence against Black people was lynching, which is hanging someone from a tree or platform using a rope. As a result of legal restrictions and violence, many Black people left their homes in the South to live in Northern and Western cities. This was called the Great Migration. (See "Rosa the Revolutionary" on page 160 for more on the Great Migration.) Black people moved to cities like San Francisco, Oakland, New York City, Philadelphia, Detroit, Washington, D.C., and Chicago.

Sadly, the violence of the South awaited them in the North and West. The migration of Blacks to Northern and Western cities angered whites there due to competition for jobs and housing. Their anger led to violence against Black people in some of these cities, reaching a new level in July 1919. The white violence against Black people was so horrible and frequent in that month that it was called the Red Summer of 1919—red for all the bloodshed and deaths.

RESISTANCE STORIES *from* BLACK HISTORY *for* KIDS

BLACK SOLDIERS FIGHT BACK

Black soldiers who fought in World War I had returned home the year before, in 1918. When facing the threat of white mobs, many of those soldiers fought back; Black veterans would not take the abuse lying down.[325] Across the country, former soldiers used their government-provided weapons training to defend their neighborhoods against vicious white mobs.[326]

In Washington, D.C., white soldiers from the war violently harmed numerous Black people after a white woman accused "Negro thugs" of attacking her.[327] In response, more white U.S. troops were sent to control the violence. Black troops requested to serve as well to protect people from the violence but were denied. In response, those soldiers purchased their own guns. An estimated five hundred firearms were sold as soon as Black soldiers were denied the opportunity to prevent violence in their neighborhoods, which prompted the police to ask gun dealers to suspend sales.[328] When the dealers complied, some Black people organized and drove to neighboring Baltimore to buy weapons and ammunition to hand out to Black people in Washington.[329] Once armed, Black soldiers and civilians patrolled their streets throughout Washington. When met with violent mobs, they fought back. When fired upon by police, they fired back as they ran for safety.

In Chicago, a white mob killed Black teenager Eugene Williams, who was sailing in Lake Michigan. Black protesters who demanded action for his death were attacked by an armed white mob, but police refused to protect the protesters.[330] The violence continued for days, but Black people protected themselves. One example involved white seventeen-year-old Clarence Metz, who attempted to harm Louis C. Washington, a Black Army lieutenant veteran. As Metz lunged with an ax handle, Washington thrust with his pocket-knife. Stabbed in the heart, Metz bled to death on the street.[331]

In response to the continued violence, Black soldiers formed militias (military forces organized by civilians) to defend their homes, neighborhoods, and people from white violence. After Williams's death, one group of Black veterans broke into a military storage facility and stole weapons that they used to beat back a white mob.[332] Blacks set up street barriers and started firing at any whites they saw; five detectives and a police officer in a squad car were fired on several times when they tried to drive into a Black neighborhood.[333]

THE FALLOUT

In all, between April and November 1919, there were approximately twenty-five riots and instances of mob violence; ninety-seven recorded lynchings; and a three-day-long massacre in Elaine, Arkansas, during which over two hundred Black men, women, and children were killed after Black sharecroppers tried to organize for better working conditions.[334]

Armed resistance led to a cruel side effect: the police, courts, and civil authorities typically arrested and prosecuted Blacks who had been trying to defend themselves; they did not arrest white rioters. African Americans refused to yield, and instead used trials, appeals, and public campaigns to right the scales of justice. Because self-defense is a human right, Black people defended that right and would continue to do so throughout the fight for their civil rights—and rightfully so.

CHAPTER 30
WHAT WILL THE NEIGHBORS THINK?

You many have heard someone use the term "Achilles' heel." It simply means a weakness that, despite one's strength, could lead to one's downfall. The term refers to a mythical Greek warrior Achilles who died in the Trojan War when he was struck in the vulnerable area of his foot by a Trojan prince.

When Achilles was a child, a legend says that his mother dipped him into the River Styx, which made him invulnerable to death. However, his mother held him by his heel, so that portion of his body did not touch the water and was not invulnerable. Achilles grew strong and became a mighty warrior, but he had a weakness: his heel. During the Cold War between the United States and the Soviet Union (led by Russia), the United States had a weakness: racism. And the warriors in the civil rights movement were wise to strike at the Achilles' heel of the United States.

What Was the Cold War?

The Cold War was a period of conflict in the second half of the twentieth century between the United States and the then-Soviet Union over the geopolitical (political decisions based on geographic factors) direction of the world.

RACISM AFTER THE WAR

After the end of World War II in 1945, the U.S. hoped to reshape the postwar world in its image. But the international attention on racial segregation was troublesome and embarrassing.[335] As the Soviet Union sought to increase its political footprint and encourage

WHAT WILL THE NEIGHBORS THINK?

nations in Africa, Asia, and Latin America to become Communist, the U.S. sought to do the opposite, encouraging them to become capitalist and prodemocratic.

The problem was that these nations were made up of people of color. The nations in Africa and Latin America had either Black people or people descended from them. This was a problem because people in those nations saw how African Americans were being treated by the very government attempting to convince them that the U.S. could be trusted to do right by them. Logically speaking, how could a nation of Black people trust the U.S. over the Soviet Union when the U.S. was actively terrorizing Black people?

Racial segregation in the use of public places and services, housing, employment, and schooling led to racial unfairness; the lynching of Black people; and Black genocide (purposefully destroying a group of people) in the destruction of whole towns like Wilmington in North Carolina, Tulsa in Oklahoma, and Rosewood in Florida. This racial terror ruined the image of American democracy throughout the world, and the U.S. government knew it. Nations around the world drew attention to this through their press coverage. A Greek newspaper noted that "America has an Achilles' heel and... the heel is quite Black."[336]

EMBARRASSMENT ON THE WORLD STAGE

In 1947, the Haitian Secretary of Agriculture Francois Georges traveled to a Biloxi, Mississippi, hotel to attend an agriculture conference.[337] He was denied his hotel reservation because of "reasons of color."[338] Georges left without attending the conference and embarrassed the U.S. in an article in a Haitian newspaper. A similar story happened in 1961, when the ambassador from the African country of Chad visited President John F. Kennedy and was refused service in a Washington, D.C., restaurant.

Events like these didn't help the U.S. in the eyes of countries they hoped to influence both politically and economically. In an attempt to do damage control—from the administration of President Harry

Truman starting in 1945—the U.S. acted to help change how it was perceived in a Cold War world.

A CHANGE IN APPROACH

In 1947, Truman warned that "the treatment which our Negroes receive is taken as a reflection of our attitudes toward all dark-skinned peoples. ... We cannot escape the fact that our civil rights record has been an issue in world politics."[339] Aware of the Achilles' heel, the National Association for the Advancement of Colored People (NAACP) published a petition, "An Appeal to the World," that same year with the United Nations (an organization formed to maintain global peace and cooperation) protesting the treatment of Black people in the U.S.[340] According to W.E.B. DuBois, the petition was not introduced in the United Nations for fear of harming the reputation of the U.S.; however, the document received extensive coverage in the domestic and foreign press.

This resulted in further harming the reputation of the United States in the world. One of the authors of the document, DuBois, said, "When will nations learn that their enemies are not usually without but within? It is not Russia that threatens the United States but Mississippi... internal injustice done to one's brothers is far more dangerous than the aggression of strangers from abroad.[341]

With these same concerns in mind, Truman's secretary of state, Dean Acheson, mentioned the need to improve the image of the U.S. in an amicus brief for the 1952 Supreme Court case Brown v. Board of Education. This case was filed by a Black man, Oliver Brown, whose daughter was denied entrance to an all-white elementary school. The brief said that "the undeniable existence of racial discrimination gives unfriendly governments the most effective kind of ammunition for their propaganda warfare... [racial discrimination] jeopardizes the effective maintenance of our moral leadership of the free and democratic nations of the world."[342]

What Is an Amicus Brief?

An amicus or amicus curiae (Latin for "friend of the court") brief is a document filed by a person about a court case under review. The person who files the brief is not a party in the case, and the brief expresses how the decision made by the court will affect other people in addition to the specific people the case concerns.

The amicus brief put pressure on the Supreme Court to rule in favor of *Brown* and made clear to the lawyers for the NAACP arguing the *Brown* case that they had the federal government on their side. The government's arguing against school segregation in previous court cases dating back to 1949 is what encouraged the *Brown* lawsuit.

The *Brown* decision, ending racial segregation in public schools, was tested under President Dwight Eisenhower with the Little Rock Nine—nine Black students who were the first to attend Central High School in Little Rock, Arkansas. Eisenhower was reluctant to enforce the court's decision for fear of angering white voters. But negative international press from Latin America, Asia, and Africa forced him to order federal troops to help the Little Rock Nine enter the school. He said that enemies of the U.S. were celebrating the failure of this event and "using it everywhere to misrepresent our whole nation."[343]

RESPONSE OF CIVIL RIGHTS LEADERSHIP

Civil rights leaders used to their advantage the fact that the world was watching. James Farmer, executive director of the civil rights organization the Congress of Racial Equality (CORE), initiated the Freedom Rides in 1961. These were bus trips made by white and Black civil rights activists, called Freedom Riders, to protest against segregated buses and bus terminals. The activists were greeted with violence from Southern white mobs and Southern police who joined in, showed approval, or looked the other way.[344] President Kennedy asked Farmer to call off the rides on the evening of a meeting with the Soviet leader Nikita Khrushchev.

However, Farmer did not. He understood the power of images and how news of the violence committed against Black people could apply pressure on the U.S. to do something about racism. Minister and activist Martin Luther King Jr. used his efforts during the civil rights movement to achieve a similar goal. By announcing protest marches to the news media, King took advantage of white violence against Black people at protest marches as a way to show the ugliness of racism through pictures and video. Through these efforts, civil rights leaders used the Achilles' heel of the United States to achieve civil rights goals for Black people.

CHAPTER 31

A NEGRO WITH A GUN

I can only imagine what it was like to live in the Jim Crow South, where racist laws required racial segregation. The disrespect as well as the dangers were traumatic. My father was born during that time in Georgia, which is in the South, but when he was three, his parents moved their family to New Jersey to leave segregation behind.

When my grandfather died, I remember looking through some of his things in the basement with my cousins and my grandmother, and we found some interesting items. But nothing was more interesting than the shotguns she found and gave to my dad to hold for safekeeping. I asked my grandmother why grandpop had shotguns. She told me that they were mostly for hunting animals, but they were also for self-defense in case they were threatened by any racist white folks.

When she told me that, it was my first introduction to the dangers Black people faced in the segregated South. I had heard the stories of the fire hoses and police dogs used on people during the civil rights movement, but my grandparents were people I knew who had experienced the sort of racism I learned about in school. I asked her if there were other Black people who had guns to hunt and defend themselves. She told me that pretty much everyone she knew had one. When I learned about Robert Williams, I wasn't surprised at all.

WHO IS ROBERT WILLIAMS?

Robert F. Williams was a civil rights activist and the leader of his local NAACP office[345] in Monroe, North Carolina, elected in 1955. Williams wasn't your "typical" civil rights leader. Unlike most civil rights leaders known throughout the nation, who believed in nonviolence even when attacked, Williams believed in self-defense, returning violence with violence.

Williams believed that Black people should arm themselves with guns to protect against violently racist white people, such as members of the Ku Klux Klan (a violent, racist group with a goal to maintain the power of white Christians). With that idea in mind, he encouraged (if not demanded) the people he recruited to join the NAACP to arm themselves. Williams's philosophy had to be put into practice when he and members of the Monroe NAACP had to defend the home of a Black doctor from Monroe—who was accused and later convicted of performing an abortion, a medical birth control procedure, on a white woman—from an angry white mob.[346]

For his stance, the NAACP suspended Williams from his leadership.[347] But he was not discouraged. When two Black children died swimming in a local creek because Black people weren't allowed in the town pool, Williams and other Black Monroe citizens protested, using their guns as protection against a white mob. When city officials realized that Williams and the others wouldn't back down, the officials allowed them to continue protesting—however, they remained under threat from the mob.

WILLIAMS FACES BACKLASH

In August 1961, the Freedom Riders[348]—Black and white civil rights activists who rode buses in the South to protest against segregation in buses and bus terminals—came to Monroe. "The Freedom Rides were first conceived in 1947 when CORE and the fellowship of Reconciliation, an interfaith fellowship group, organized an interracial bus ride across state lines to test a Supreme Court decision that declared segregation on interstate buses unconstitutional." On this occasion, racist agitators and terrorists appeared in Monroe to attack both the Freedom Riders and Robert Williams. The racist mob was made up of thousands of people from all over the South, and they were largely invited by white citizens of Monroe who were looking for a fight with Williams and his supporters.

A riot occurred at the local courthouse during which this mob attacked children they believed to be protesters. Afterward, fed up with racism and oppression, hundreds of Black citizens from various towns surrounding Monroe came to Williams's home to defend it. They had heard rumors that the mob and the Ku Klux Klan were on their way to kill Williams.[349] A white couple near Williams's home was taken hostage (kidnapped and held by force) by these local Black residents for fear they were attempting to kill Williams.

Once the white mob arrived at Williams's home, a shootout ensued between them and the Black residents defending Williams. Williams was alerted that the state police were on their way to arrest him. But he and his family escaped before the police arrived. They went first to Greensboro, North Carolina, and then to New York City. Some reports say this was by way of a friend finding them in the woods, and others say it was by way of a funeral hearse retrieving them from their home.[350]

Charged for kidnapping the white couple, Williams fled the United States and went to Cuba as a guest of Fidel Castro, the Communist leader of Cuba at the time. With Castro's support, Williams began broadcasting a weekly radio program, "Radio Free Dixie," that reached thousands of Black listeners in the United States despite U.S. government efforts to scramble the radio signal.[351] After traveling the world denouncing racism, colonialism, and the war in Vietnam, Williams returned to the United States in 1969 and all charges against[352] him from the 1961 event were dropped.

CHAPTER 32

NEGROES WITH GUNS

An often-promoted theme of the civil rights movement is the philosophy of nonviolent protests. Martin Luther King Jr. believed in this philosophy to attract national and international support for the civil rights of Black people in the United States.

To be clear, no one person or group associated with that movement promoted violence or protesting by violent means. However, some did promote self-defense when provoked or attacked by white people, or angry mobs or individuals, or even law enforcement.

One group that advocated for the Black use of self-defense, while adhering to the ideas of nonviolence, was the Deacons for Defense and Justice, led by Earnest Thomas, Frederick Douglass Kirkpatrick, and Charles Sims.

THE DEACONS FOR DEFENSE AND JUSTICE

The Deacons for Defense and Justice was organized in Jonestown, Louisiana, in March 1965.[353] The group consisted of Black people who served as church deacons—who assist ministers and help members of the church—in Christian churches; the group's goal was to protect both individuals and civil rights groups from attacks by the Ku Klux Klan (a violent, racist group with a goal to maintain the power of white Christians).

A 1965 *New York Times* article defined the group as "the newest of the Negro civil rights organizations... an armed, semi-secret, loosely organized federation... a tough-minded league of Negroes, formed to defend members of their race from white terrorism."[354]

This group continued a tradition of armed resistance seen a few years earlier in the Monroe, North Carolina, chapter of the NAACP and its leader Robert Williams. NAACP members had armed themselves with guns to defend the Black residents of Monroe from attacks from white people.[355] (See "A Negro with a Gun" on page 136 for more on Robert Williams.)

What Was COINTELPRO?

The Counterintelligence Program, or COINTELPRO, was a project of the Federal Bureau of Investigation (FBI), a government agency that enforces U.S. law. The program was designed to monitor and disrupt the activities of the Communist Party in the United States. But it expanded to include targeting so-called Black extremist groups, such as the Southern Christian Leadership Conference of Martin Luther King Jr., the Nation of Islam and Malcolm X, and the Black Panther Party for Self-Defense (later called the Black Panther Party) under the leadership of Bobby Seale and Huey Newton. (See "How the Kids Got Free Breakfast" on page 156 for more about COINTELPRO.)

THE WORK OF THE DEACONS FOR DEFENSE

An example of how the Deacons for Defense served Black people occurred on a July night in 1965, when a twenty-five-car motorcade of Ku Klux Klansmen traveled through a Black neighborhood in Bogalusa, Louisiana. The Klansmen intimidated and terrorized Black residents by yelling racial slurs, including the n-word, exposing their guns, and even shooting their guns in the air. Some Klansmen began firing their guns into random Black homes. Normally, Black families wouldn't fight back out of fear of further harm from hate groups.[356]

However, the Black residents of this neighborhood returned the bullets of Klansmen with bullets of their own. As a result of residents firing back, the Klansmen left the neighborhood immediately.[357] The Deacons led the defense of the neighborhood.

The group would go on to defend Black neighborhoods throughout the South, in states like Louisiana, Alabama, Mississippi,

Arkansas, and Texas. While the group believed in the philosophy of nonviolence to bring about change on behalf of Black civil rights, its mission was to defend Black people, with violence, if necessary. Protected by the right to bear arms as stated in the U.S. Constitution, the Deacons operated within the law.[358]

The group gained national attention for protecting civil rights marchers, including activists Martin Luther King Jr. and Stokely Carmichael (later known as Kwame Ture) during the March Against Fear in 1966. This march was inspired by civil rights leader James Meredith, who had been shot and injured earlier in that march on the road from Memphis, Tennessee, to Jackson, Mississippi, to promote voting rights for Black people.

The March Against Fear started from the place where Meredith had been shot and was organized by civil rights activists from the Southern Christian Leadership Congress, CORE, and the Student Nonviolent Coordinating Committee (SNCC), who continued the work of Meredith. Unfortunately, the relevance of the Deacons declined due to interference and disruption by the FBI's COINTELPRO.

BY THE NUMBERS: THE SUPER SIX*

NAACP (1909)

National Association for the Advancement of Colored People: Published the *Crisis* magazine led by cofounder W. E. B. DuBois and its Legal Defense Fund; led civil rights cases in the courts.

NUL (1910)

National Urban League: Counseled Black migrants in urban areas in the North as well as assisted in training Blacks to provide educational and increased employment opportunities in industry.

BSCP (1925)

Brotherhood of Sleeping Car Porters: Led by A. Philip Randolph, who secured recognition as a union for Black workers and a union contract, affording Randolph the ability to fight against segregation in other ways.

CORE (1942)

Congress for Racial Equality: Organized direct nonviolent actions to achieve racial justice, including promoting interstate bus travel to test a Supreme Court ruling.

SCLC (1957)

Southern Christian Leadership Conference: Led by Martin Luther King Jr.; participated in boycotts, protests, and marches across the southern United States.

SNCC (1960)

Student Nonviolent Coordinating Committee: Led by John Lewis and Stokely Carmichael (later known as Kwame Ture); participated in protests and marches during the civil rights movement.

* "National Urban League," Stanford University, September 39, 1910, https://kinginstitute.stanford.edu/encyclopedia/national-urban-league.

RESISTANCE STORIES *from* BLACK HISTORY *for* KIDS

CHAPTER 33
THE KING'S SPEECH

Martin Luther King Jr.'s "I Have a Dream" speech may be the most well-known, and important, speech in U.S. history. When I had to recite a part of that speech in second grade, my portion was a well-known and popular part as opposed to the beginning of the speech that is less known and, therefore, less popular. Looking back now, I think that my lack of familiarity and the world's lack of familiarity with the earlier potion of the speech wasn't an accident but was intentional.

Who Was Martin Luther King Jr.?

Martin Luther King Jr. was a Christian minister with a doctorate degree in theology (the study of religion) who led numerous civil rights protests and marches during the civil rights movement. For many, King was the face of the movement. He's known for leading the Montgomery bus boycott in Montgomery, Alabama; his "I Have a Dream" speech; his letter from a Birmingham jail; and winning the Nobel Peace Prize. But his two biggest accomplishments are the role he played in encouraging the U.S. government to enact the Civil Rights Act of 1964 and the Voting Rights Act of 1965.

THE MANIPULATION OF KING

On November 2, 1983, President Ronald Reagan signed a bill into law that created the national holiday to honor King. However, Reagan originally opposed the holiday, claiming cost concerns.[359] Reagan even insulted King, hinting that he had Communist ties. For that, he apologized to King's widow, Coretta Scott King. In the end, Reagan used the holiday to dilute King's message.

Reagan wasn't a friend to civil rights for Blacks, speaking out against the Civil Rights Act of 1964 and the Voting Rights Act of 1965—the results of King's activism.[360] But in the fall of 1983, Reagan changed his position, claiming that his previous point of view was based "on an image [of King], not reality."[361] He used King's 1963 "I Have a Dream" speech to turn King into a symbol of color blindness. Reagan quoted the following words from King's speech in his announcement about Martin Luther King Jr. Day (MLK Day): "I have a dream that my four little children will one day live in a nation where they will not be judged by the color of their skin but by the content of their character."

What Is Color Blindness?

Color blindness is the concept of not seeing color as a means of being fair and just. The problem with this is that it is insensitive and dismissive of the experiences of people of color, particularly Black people. When Black people are viewed and treated with a color-blind mind-set, these actions fail to account for the history of systemic racism imposed on people of color in a white supremacist society.

WHAT'S IGNORED IN KING'S SPEECH

The quote above is one of the most often recited portions of King's speech. This is because it's the safest part of his speech. It downplays what's considered to be the more extreme aspects of King's message in favor of a friendlier, less confrontational message that fails to say what King actually said: ridiculing America's racism, capitalism, and militarism, in addition to offering an analysis of the U.S. condition because of those phenomena. King offered his analysis and judgment of the United States in the "I Have a Dream" speech, but those observations were conveniently left out by Reagan in his remarks about Martin Luther King Day and by teachers nationwide every MLK Day. In that speech, King also said:

> This is not time to engage in the luxury of cooling off or to take the tranquilizing drug of gradualism. Now is the time to make real the promise of democracy. It would be fatal for the nation to overlook the urgency of the moment and to underestimate the determination of its colored citizens.
>
> Those who hope that the colored Americans needed to blow off steam and will now be content will have a rude awakening if the nation returns to business as usual. There will be neither rest nor tranquility in America until the colored citizen is granted his citizenship rights. The whirlwinds of revolt will continue to shake the foundations of our nation until the bright day of justice emerges.

You don't generally hear these words on MLK Day, which has become a day of service. Serving and volunteering in your community of course is important. King's message was that people need to treat people better, but it was in the context of a society rooted in white settler colonialism in which Indigenous people had their land taken away from them and were murdered, and Africans were kidnapped, enslaved in a foreign land, and denied their humanity when enslaved and "emancipated." King's message challenged the white power structure to grant Black people their citizenship rights or else there would be "neither rest nor [peacefulness] in America."

AN UNFILTERED KING

King was antiwar because he wanted peace throughout the world. He also understood that a government invested in war, via tax dollars, was a government that wasn't investing in helping the poor.[362] King said, "A nation that continues year after year to spend more money on military defense than on programs of social uplift is approaching spiritual death."[363]

King recognized that the poor weren't poor because of personal failures; instead, poverty was the result of capitalism. Therefore, King was anti-capitalist, saying that the trouble with capitalism is that "capitalism does not permit an even flow of economic resources... a small privileged few are rich beyond conscience, and almost all others are doomed to be poor at some level."[364]

King, of course, was also antiracist. He said, "The doctrine of white supremacy was embedded in every textbook and preached in practically every pulpit" and "a structural part of the culture."[365] King also said, "If America does not respond creatively to the challenge to banish racism, some future historian will have to say, that a great civilization died because it lacked the soul and commitment to make justice a reality for all men."[366]

Because of words like those, 63 percent of Americans had an unfavorable view of King in 1966.[367] In 1968, King was shot and killed, and 31 percent of Americans at that time said that King brought on his assassination.[368] Maybe King's words were considered too extreme and dangerous and are why President Reagan and numerous congressmen weren't in favor of a holiday for King. By the time King's memorial opened in Washington, D.C., in 2011, 94 percent of Americans had a favorable view of him. Perhaps most of them have not read or heard King's "revolutionary" speech. Rather, they've been given an image of King, not the reality.

CHAPTER 34

FROM CIVIL RIGHTS TO HUMAN RIGHTS

When I was nine years old, my dad took me to see director Spike Lee's *Malcolm X* at the movie theater. Little did I know that the movie was three hours long. But still, I was focused the whole time. I remember asking my dad questions and being caught up in the story of Brother el-Shabazz. The actor Denzel Washington did a great job bringing Brother el-Shabazz's life to light. The movie was my first in-depth look at el-Hajj Malik el-Shabazz (1925–1965).

I had heard of him before, as Malcolm X, but always juxtaposed with minister and activist Martin Luther King Jr. as the more radical of the two. But after seeing the film, I thought of him not as extreme but as revolutionary. I remember my former Spanish teacher sharing her belief that el-Shabazz was violent. She said so in the classroom. I doubt anyone else really heard her or even cared; most of the people in my class were white and unaware of the person I knew el-Shabazz to be.

I remember telling my mom about this, and she spoke with that teacher, but that's another story. Looking back, my former teacher probably learned that el-Shabazz appeared angry and confrontational. As she told my mother, she was taught that he was hateful. Many people probably learn that el-Shabazz was hateful due to his association with the Nation of Islam. But that's not the whole story of el-Shabazz.

WHAT IS THE NATION OF ISLAM?

The Nation of Islam is a Black separatist group—meaning they want Black people to have their own nation where they can govern themselves. Why they appeared hateful during el-Shabazz's time with them was due to their rejection of white superiority and supremacy in the name of Black pride and Black nationalism. That was displayed by bold words that spoke out about the actions of whites throughout American history and their effects. The group practiced elements of Islam, but it was not a traditional Islamic religious group.

While the Nation of Islam leadership used hateful language, el-Shabazz wasn't hateful; he simply loved Black people enough not to withhold from Black people the raw truth about racism and white supremacy or the white power structure. His love for Black people was pure, so much so that he left the Nation of Islam due to actions he thought were contrary to what he believed the Nation stood for.

He left the Nation. He went on his own spiritual journey and became a traditional Muslim; he abandoned many of the Nation's beliefs and adopted his own. His truth became one that acknowledged the Islamic religion as the only way white, Black, and all other peoples of color could overcome the violence of racism and white supremacy.

The Many Names of Malcolm X

Malcolm X was born as Malcolm Little. When he joined the Nation of Islam, he changed his name to Malcolm X, the "X" standing for the name of his African ancestors unknown to him. The Nation was a Black religious organization rooted in the Islamic faith and promoted Black nationalism (which calls for empowering Black people, developing Black identity and community, and forming a separate Black nation). When he made a pilgrimage to the Muslim holy city of Mecca, as required by Islam, Malcolm X changed his name to el-Hajj Malik el-Shabazz. This book refers to him by that final name he chose for himself.

FROM MECCA TO AFRICA

After his break from the Nation of Islam in 1964, el-Shabazz made a pilgrimage to Mecca, in Saudi Arabia. He described Mecca: "Never have I witnessed such sincere hospitality and the overwhelming spirit of true brotherhood as is practiced by people of all colors and races here in this ancient holy land, the home of Abraham, Muhammad, and all the other prophets of the Holy Scriptures. For the past week I have been utterly speechless and spellbound by the graciousness I see displayed all around me by people of all colors."[369]

When he returned to the United States, el-Shabazz created the Organization for Afro-American Unity designed to work with other Black leaders and organizations to start a movement for the human rights of Black people. El-Shabazz focused on bringing the cause of Black people in the United States to the attention of international community. He submitted an eight-page report to thirty-three heads of African states, asking them to help with the cause of African people in the United States.

He wrote: "Our [Black people] problem is your problem. No matter how much independence Africans get here on the mother continent, unless you wear your national dress at all times, when you visit America, you may be mistaken for one of us and suffer the same psychological humiliation and physical mutilation that is an everyday occurrence in our lives."[370] This was true. For example, sociologist John David Skrentny detailed how the ambassador from Chad who visited President John F. Kennedy in 1961 was "thrown on [his] rear end as a result of entering the Bonnie Brae (a white only) restaurant on Route 40."[371] Later in the report, el-Shabazz wrote:

The Organization of Afro-American Unity, in cooperation with a coalition of other Negro leaders and organizations, has decided to elevate our freedom struggle above the domestic level of civil rights. We intend to "internationalize" it by placing it at the level of human rights. Our freedom struggle for human dignity is no longer confined to the domestic jurisdiction of the United States government. We beseech the independent African states to help us bring our problem before the United Nations, on the grounds that the United States government is morally incapable of protecting the lives and the property of 22 million African Americans. And on the grounds that our deteriorating plight is definitely becoming a threat to world peace.[372]

WHY IT MATTERS TODAY

El-Shabazz was aware of the definition the United Nations (an organization formed to maintain global peace and cooperation) gave of genocide—loosely described as "acts committed with intent to destroy, in whole or in part, a national, ethnic, racial, or religious group."[373] With the help of the nations of Africa he petitioned, he was prepared to show how genocide was happening to Black people in the United States.

El-Shabazz understood that collaboration among Black people internationally before the United Nations was the way to pressure the United States to repair the harm it did to or allowed to be done to Black people. To attain that goal, he understood the importance of refocusing the fight from civil rights for Black people as Americans to human rights as citizens of the world. In his 1964 speech "The Ballot or the Bullet," el-Shabazz said:

> You can take Uncle Sam before a world court. But the only level you can do it on is the level of human rights. Civil rights keeps you under his restrictions, under his jurisdiction.... Human rights are your God-given rights. Human rights are the rights that are recognized by all nations of this earth. And any time anyone violates your human rights, you can take them to the world court.[374]

The actions of el-Shabazz are relevant today, considering the unjust killings of Black people in the United States and around the world. In 2020, the United Nations Human Rights Council led efforts to address systemic racism of law enforcement groups against people of African descent. The Council recommended establishing an independent international commission to do the following:

RESISTANCE STORIES *from* BLACK HISTORY *for* KIDS

Establish the facts and circumstances relating to the systemic racism, alleged violations of international human rights law, and abuses against Africans and people of African descent in the United States of America and other parts of the world recently affected by law enforcement agencies, especially those incidents that resulted in the deaths of Africans and of people of African descent, with a view to bringing perpetrators to justice [and] calls upon the government of the United States of America and other parts of the world recently affected, and all relevant parties to cooperate fully with the commission of inquiry.[375]

In 2021, after an extensive investigation into the matter, the Human Rights Council released its report and recommendations for destroying systemic racism around the world. It seems like el-Shabazz's message and methods still remain relevant some sixty years later.

CHAPTER 35

BLACK PANTHERS AROUND THE WORLD

As a kid, I had an "old soul" personality. I'd often hear people say about me, "He's been here before." That's probably because of my taste in music. As a kid, I loved Michael Jackson and MC Hammer. But as a preteen and teen, I graduated to Maze featuring Frankie Beverly, Roy Ayers and Ubiquity, James Brown, War, and my all-time favorite Earth, Wind & Fire. But I also loved George Clinton's bands Parliament and Funkadelic. Add Parliament and Funkadelic together and that makes P-Funk.

High school marked a very heavy P-Funk phase for me. I consumed every album from both Parliament and Funkadelic. Accompanying the wonderful music was the album art, which was so dope. Just about every album cover had great art, but the album cover that stood out to me the most, and which I think is most iconic (what best symbolizes someone or something that is influential), is the art from the album *Uncle Jam Wants You*. It's simply a picture of George Clinton dressed in a soldier's uniform, sitting in a wicker chair with the one nation under a groove flag behind him, a flashlight to his right, and a bop gun to his left.

I apologize if you don't get the significance of the flag, flashlight, or bop gun—they each refer to songs in the P-Funk catalog. But what you should pay attention to is the significance of the wicker chair. Clinton sitting in that chair (in a soldier's uniform) was a tribute to Huey Newton, cofounder of the Black Panthers. There is an iconic picture of Huey Newton sitting in a wicker chair with a gun in his right hand and a spear in his left. The picture is a clear indicator that he and the Panthers were about action—but action for the self-defense of Black people.

THE PURPOSE OF THE BLACK PANTHERS

The Black Panther Party for Self-Defense (later called the Black Panther Party) was one of the most militant groups to emerge out of the rise of social-political movements in the U.S. during the 1960s. It was organized when many Black people—particularly students and other youth—had become unhappy with the civil rights movement's primary tactic of nonviolence.[376]

Founded in Oakland, California, by Huey Newton and Bobby Seale in October 1966, the group called for full employment for Black people, adequate housing for all, a truthful education for Black children, the end of police brutality against Black people, and other demands as set forth in its ten-point program. However, the group is most remembered for asserting their Second Amendment rights—the right to bear arms—and openly carry guns to protect themselves and Black people from police brutality.

The black panther was the symbol of the Lowndes County Freedom Organization, formed by the SNCC in Alabama in 1965.[377] SNCC had selected the black panther because it is known to be an animal that never makes an unprovoked attack but will defend itself forcefully when attacked, and this was symbolic of what the Black Panther Party of Self-Defense stood for.[378]

Although the Black Panthers were based in the United States, mainly in urban centers where Black people lived, their influence was international, reaching countries in Africa, the Middle East, and even the South Pacific. The organization's writings were read by Black groups looking to liberate themselves, and its structure was a model for Black groups looking to organize against oppression. This is especially true for Black people in Israel.

THE ISRAELI BLACK PANTHER PARTY

In 1969, Israeli activists and politicians Sa'adia Marciano and Charlie Biton started meeting to discuss North African Jews' experiences of joblessness, police beatings, housing and education discrimination, and exclusion from government political offices and positions.[379] When they read about antiracist liberation movements in other countries, they decided in 1971 to name the group they founded the Israeli Black Panther Party (IBPP). They used the Black Panthers' well-recognized name to "make the government take this group seriously" and to draw national attention to the fact that Israeli discrimination against them was similar to the experiences of African Americans. They also adopted the Black Panthers' model for protesting and organizing.[380]

The IBPP used the term Mizrahi Jews (Arab Jews) to bring national attention to this group's oppression. The British discriminated against Arab Jews when they controlled Palestine from 1920 to 1948. Ashkenazi (European) Jews were favored over Mizrahi Jews, who were viewed as "primitive" and "savage."[381]

Using the Black Panther model of community self-empowerment, the IBPP also addressed access to basic needs like food and clothing by engaging in creative activities such as "liberating" milk bottles from milk trucks in middle-class neighborhoods to give to poor families.[382] In 1973, the IBPP became a political party and Biton was elected to the Israeli Parliament in 1977, where he served until 1992.[383] Although the IBPP disbanded in 1977, its lasting legacy was the establishment of the Mizrahi as a political force with a right to speak out.[384]

BLACK PANTHERS AMONG AUSTRALIAN ABORIGINES

The Australian Black Panther Party was first formed in December 1971 under the leadership of Denis Walker and Sam Watson. They declared they would be "the vanguard for all depressed people, and in Australia the Aboriginals are the most depressed of all."[385] However, interest in the Panthers in Australia dates back to 1968, when some Aboriginal activists, specifically the younger generation living in capital cities, had begun to take an interest in the idea of Black power and the activities of the Black Panther Party.[386]

RESISTANCE STORIES *from* BLACK HISTORY *for* KIDS

Inspired by the example of the American Black Panther's community survival programs, they developed the free Aboriginal Medical Service and Aboriginal Legal Service programs, housing projects, and the National Black Theatre.[387] The Aboriginal Housing Company was founded in 1972 to provide housing for the Aboriginal community and still provides this service today.[388]

When scholars have tried to document the ways in which the Black Panther Party inspired activists throughout the world, they typically looked to those international groups that adopted the Panther name or their model. The Aboriginal Medical and Legal services, however, at least hint at the possibility that the global role of the Black Panther Party is much bigger than previously thought.[389]

CHAPTER 36

HOW THE KIDS GOT FREE BREAKFAST

As an educator, I understand the importance of a young person having a nutritious breakfast before school and lunch during school. Research shows that eating and eating healthy food are connected to academic performance.[390] Plus, I know students are hungry because young people are growing. You may be hungry reading this.

As a growing young person, you consume food regularly. I know because I sometimes treated my Advanced Placement U.S. History students, who are now in college, to Dunkin' Donuts and Chick-fil-A on random Fridays. The doughnut holes and mini chicken sandwiches don't last long at all. When I taught middle school, I would have fruit in my homeroom for students and I offered some during first period. I knew that hungry students couldn't focus. Hungry students may be sleepy students or even hangry students. If I didn't know before becoming an educator, I learned how important breakfast was for kids.

Free breakfast is now one of the U.S. government's largest aid programs, offering free meals to children whose families are below the poverty line.[391] Participation in the federally funded School Breakfast Program has slowly but steadily grown over the years: 1970: 0.5 million children; 1980: 3.6 million children; 1990: 4 million children; 2000: 7.5 million children; 2010: 11.67 million children; and 2016: 14.57 million children.[392]

Most people would thank their local congressman or those politicians who came before for the program. The truth is, those thankful for this program owe a major debt of gratitude not to the federal government or one specific politician. They owe thanks to the Black Panther Party.

HOW THE PROGRAM STARTED

A School Breakfast Program started in 1966 with a small and unpopular two-year pilot program conceived and championed by Kentucky Congressman Carl Perkins. He was concerned about the plight of children in rural areas who got up early to work in the fields with their parents and arrived to school hungry after long bus rides.[393] As the U.S. Department of Agriculture started the program, the Black Panther Party founded its own Free Breakfast for School Children Program for poor Black children. (See "Black Panthers around the World" on page 152 for more on the Black Panther Party for Self-Defense.)

Because this program was limited to rural schools, the Panthers created their program for the young people in their community. They started the program with St. Augustine's Church, an Episcopal church in Oakland, California. Local businesses donated supplies like grits, eggs, toast, and milk, and supporters across the country pitched in to make breakfast go further.[394] By the end of 1969, the program had spread to Panther chapters in twenty-three cities, feeding over twenty thousand poor Black children. In a 1969 hearing in the U.S. Senate, part of the U.S. Congress, the person running the national School Breakfast Program admitted that the Panthers fed more poor schoolchildren than the State of California did.[395]

The Black Panthers' reasoning was simple: hunger and poverty made it difficult for many poor Black children to learn in school.[396] The Panthers said that the government was supposed to be fighting poverty by feeding and taking care of people, but that wasn't happening in the Black community, so they were going to.[397] The breakfast program was part of the Panthers' community survival programs, which were designed to meet the unique needs of the Black community until the revolution. Some of these programs included a free escort program for senior citizens, a monthly bus to visit loved ones in prisons, and the establishment of thirteen medical clinics across the country.[398]

OPPOSITION TO THE PROGRAM

While the Panthers breakfast program got the attention of Black families in need, it also got the attention of J. Edgar Hoover, the director of the Federal Bureau of Investigation, or FBI (a government agency that enforces U.S. law). He stated that because of its free breakfast program, the Panthers were "the greatest threat to the internal security of the [United States]."[399]

Hoover was an enemy of the civil rights movement and of Black leaders who called out the United States for its treatment of Black people. This is well documented by the FBI itself. His counterintelligence program (COINTELPRO) was known for spying on, disrupting, and harassing Black leaders as well as civil rights and Black liberation organizations and their movements. The program operated from 1956 (during the emergence of civil rights leaders Martin Luther King Jr. and el-Hajj Malik el-Shabazz) to 1971. You can find out more about the program by visiting "The Vault" library section of the FBI website.

Hoover sabotaged the breakfast program. According to FBI records, one FBI head informed agents in San Francisco: "The BPP is not engaged in the Breakfast for Children Program for humanitarian reasons [but for others], including their efforts to create an image of civility, assume community control of Negroes, and to fill adolescent children with their insidious poison."[400] COINTELPRO efforts to interfere with the program's operations included harassment of church leaders who hosted daily meals, questioning and occasionally arresting youth and Party members who attended or volunteered for meals, citations from the public health department for minor issues, and sometimes physical destruction of the food itself.[401]

According to Panther Chief of Staff David Hilliard, who oversaw the expansion of Panther service work, "Police raided the Breakfast for Children Program, ransacked food storage facilities, destroyed kitchen equipment, and attempted to disrupt relations between the Black Panthers and local business owners and community advocates, whose contributions made the programs possible."[402] Hoover unreasonably defended FBI attempts to destroy the program because [he believed] it was "potentially the greatest threat to efforts by authorities to destroy what it [the Black Panther Party] stands for."[403] In other words, the breakfast program threatened the government's goal to damage the reputation of the Black Panthers.

Those police raids as well as internal fights, partly because of interference by CONTELPRO, led to the end of the Free Breakfast for School Children Program in the early 1970s. However, the Panther's program helped spotlight the issue of poor children needing nutritious meals; Congress expanded the breakfast program to all public schools in 1975.

WHERE CREDIT IS DUE

Some people don't give the Black Panthers credit for the government breakfast program.[404] The truth is that the Panthers do deserve much credit for their work feeding children and serving as an inspiration for the expansion of the breakfast program in 1975.

If for no other reason, expansion of the government program was one way to prevent groups like the Black Panthers from building programs addressing the racism experienced by Black people nationwide. But the work of the Panthers is another example of how thinking of liberation on behalf of Black people, by Black people, not only helps Black people but also helps all people.

CHAPTER 37

ROSA THE REVOLUTIONARY

The Great Migration marks the period in American history when Black people from the Southern (and former Confederate) states migrated to the North in the quest for freedom, jobs, and social justice. This established new patterns of race, class, and ethnic relations in American culture, society, and politics.[405] A total of anywhere between four million and six million African American people migrated between 1910 and 1970. One couple who did so were my own grandparents, Joseph and Rubie Lee Miller.

Both were from Attapulgus, Georgia, a town close to the border of Georgia and Florida. My father and two of his siblings were born there. I got a chance to visit when I was ten years old. Like other Black people, my grandparents left home in the late 1950s in search of better opportunities for themselves and their children. The reality for many Black people was that better opportunities meant leaving the Jim Crow South, where racist laws led to segregation and discrimination.

When Grandpop Joseph couldn't find work in Ohio, where he first traveled, he tried New Jersey on the recommendation of friends. A few months later, he sent for Grandmom and the kids, my dad and his siblings. The racism they encountered had to be bad for them to leave the only home they ever knew. It was; racism is a terror. But the truth is that Black folk learned that racism existed in the North, just like it did in the South. It's something Rosa Parks found out for herself.

BEFORE PARKS'S MOVE NORTH

In 1957, Rosa Parks, along with her husband and mother, moved to Detroit, Michigan. But before she did, she was involved in a protest where she refused to move to the back of a bus. This protest was the start of the Montgomery bus boycott and the civil rights movement. Sadly, the truth behind Parks protest was omitted in exchange for a watered-down story.

What really happened was that the NAACP in Montgomery, Alabama, had been seeking a test case to challenge the segregated bus system. The common belief was that the organization considered fifteen-year-old Claudette Colvin when she was arrested for violating the bus segregation rules on March 2, 1955, but a single, pregnant teenager did not strike the NAACP as a sympathetic-enough figure.[406] Colvin didn't become pregnant until after challenging bus segregation in Montgomery. But more importantly, Colvin and Parks were part of a tradition of challengers of bus segregation in Montgomery—including Viola White. She refused to give up her seat in 1944 and was arrested. When she decided to press her case, police raped her daughter. Then the state tied up her appeal and never let it come to court.[407] Three other Black women were arrested for the same action in the following months; but it was only with the arrest of Rosa Parks on December 1, 1955, that was the final insult.

Why Rosa Parks? Well, the popular story says it's because Parks was a respectable member of the community. That unlike Colvin, Parks was married. Also, Parks was a civil rights activist; both she and her husband were members of the Montgomery NAACP. She joined in the 1940s and was later elected secretary of the Montgomery chapter. She was an adviser of its youth group, and in the summer of 1955, she participated in a civil rights training workshop at the Highlander Folk School in Tennessee.[408] While those facts are true, that's not why she was "chosen." If Colvin and others like 18-year-old Mary Louise Smith hadn't refused to give up their seats, Black Montgomery residents might not have been at the breaking point when Rosa Parks was arrested on December 1.[409] Movements like the Civil Rights Movement don't happen with the first violation of injustice but rather when injustices build up to the point of intolerance.

When Parks refused to give up her seat, it wasn't planned for that day, but there was a plan to do it one day. Parks never sat at the front of the bus. She was sitting at the front of the colored section of the bus when she refused to give up her seat.[410] The front of the colored section was reserved for white people when the white section was full, and on the day she refused to give up her seat, the white section was full.

Why this case was so effective is because had she sat at the very front of the bus, it would have invited confrontation—enabling racists to say that such an act was done because of the influence or at the instruction of outside agitators. Whites would use the idea that protests were sparked by outside revolutionaries to make the case that most Black people were OK with segregation. But if such a protest was unplanned and not confrontational on its face, the only ammunition the opponents of racial justice would have was their racism.

Parks's story was told differently though (by the media or maybe the U.S. government)—with the claim that she sat at the front of the bus—for the sake of reducing racism to something that is an individual evil as opposed to what it is: a systemic evil. What makes racism a systemic evil, in the case of Parks, is that there was a colored section of the bus. This wasn't simply because the bus company did it. Rather the bus company did it because Jim Crow segregation policy made it legal. The existence of Jim Crow laws clearly shows racism as something systemic, rather than racism being something individuals simply did. For Parks, as shown by this quote, it was an evil she encountered daily: "My resistance to being mistreated on the buses and anywhere else was just a regular thing with me and not just that day."[411]

THE DETROIT YEARS

For the next three hundred eighty-one days after her protest, Parks faced stubbornness from city officials, police harassment, and threats from white supremacists, yet she fought to ensure the success of the Montgomery bus boycott. After the boycott ended,

Parks struggled to find work in Montgomery and continued to receive death threats because of her activism.[412] The Parks family chose to leave Montgomery and settle in Detroit.

Her description of Detroit: the northern promised land that wasn't.[413] Although the visible harm of Jim Crow was gone—the separate drinking fountains, buses, elevators, and lunch counters—Parks didn't find too much difference between race relations in Detroit and Montgomery, saying, "I don't feel a great deal of difference here, personally.... Housing segregation is just as bad, and it seems more noticeable in the large cities."[414] With that, she got to work as a civil rights activist as she had in Montgomery.

Parks led an NAACP march to protest housing discrimination, spoke at civil rights luncheons, and marched with Martin Luther King Jr. in Detroit's 1963 Walk to Freedom, which drew nearly two hundred thousand people.[415] She found work and accepted a job sewing aprons and skirts for ten hours a day, receiving 75 cents for every piece she completed.

She volunteered for the campaign of the late Black Congressman John Conyers, helping him get elected with a visit from King that she brought about on Conyers's behalf. Conyers hired Parks to attend to the needs of the people in his district, a job she held from 1965 to 1988; she visited schools, hospitals, senior citizen facilities, and community meetings, and kept Conyers informed of community concerns and activism.[416] Taking up a variety of urban social issues, Parks heard people's problems and filled in for Conyers at rallies and other public events.[417]

RACISM CAN LIVE ANYWHERE

Despite the popular belief that Parks, and King, were beloved outside the South by the early 1960s, they were regularly called Communists for their support of open housing and desegregated schools in the North. Parks continued to receive hate mail and hate calls well into the 1970s in Detroit.[418] One 1972 letter from Indiana made clear the writer's objections to her move North: "Why didn't you stay down South? The North sure doesn't want you up here. You are the biggest woman troublemaker ever."[419]

In cities like Detroit, public officials regularly rejected Black demands with the charge that "this is not the South." They meant to ignore a growing civil rights movement around housing, schools, jobs, and police brutality.[420] Saying that crime, poverty, and failing schools were a result of a cultural defects as opposed to systemic racism enabled Northern whites to claim they didn't understand the purpose of the civil rights movement in the first place.

But Parks's move to a Northern ghetto in 1957 and her activism related to school and housing segregation, welfare, and police brutality in the 1960s and 1970s prove that racism has no home base—racism is everywhere and must be challenged everywhere for democracy to be available to all.

CHAPTER 38

MANDELA THE TERRORIST

For many of you, 1990 may sound like hundreds of years ago. But for me, 1990 can sometimes feel like yesterday. I still remember the yellow wallpaper in my bedroom, where my television was, and the Nintendo in my room.

When I wasn't playing video games, I'd watch some TV. Sometimes I'd watch the news. One event I remember watching happened a month after my seventh birthday: Nelson Mandela, the South African freedom fighter against apartheid, was released from prison.

American Racism: An Idol of Afrikaners

America's brand of racism served as an inspiration to other racists around the world, including the Afrikaners of South Africa. Apartheid in South Africa developed partly as a way to advance racial social engineering, inspired by the American goal of curing social ills by way of experimentation rooted in eugenic thinking.[421] Eugenics is the scientifically inaccurate theory that humans can be improved by allowing only certain people to have children; this idea was fueled by the outcomes of enslavement and the fear of interracial relationships between white and Black people.

APARTHEID AND NELSON MANDELA

Apartheid (meaning "apartness" in Afrikaans) was the legal system for racial separation in South Africa from 1948 until 1994.[422] Afrikaans was the language spoken by Afrikaners (which means "Africans" in Dutch)—a South African ethnic group descended from seventeenth-century Dutch, German, and French settlers in South Africa.[423] The institution of apartheid was developed so that Afrikaners (white settlers), rather than African people, could concentrate and maintain political and economic control of South Africa.

The Popular Registration Act of 1950 first classified all South Africans into three categories: bantu (Blacks), colored (those of mixed race), and white. This law specified where people could live, what jobs they could have, what facilities they could use, where they could go to school, and whom they could have social contact with, according to their category.[424]

Afrikaners aimed to use apartheid, a system similar to Jim Crow, to establish (and maintain) South Africa as a white man's country—this was a white settler colonial project, with white settlers, from a European country, colonizing a territory that was not theirs—but various African groups chose to fight back against this racist domination of African people. One such group was the African National Congress (ANC), a Black nationalist organization founded in 1912 to fight for the rights of Black South Africans. Its sole purpose became eliminating the apartheid system once that was instituted in South Africa.

In 1944, a college graduate named Nelson Mandela joined the ANC, developing its youth league and rising through the ranks as volunteer-in-chief of the ANC's Defiance Campaign. This group engaged in civil disobedience (similar to the actions of Martin Luther King Jr. and Rosa Parks)[425] to promote Black rights. Mandela later became commander in chief of the armed wing of the ANC known as uMkhonto we Sizwe (Spear of the Nation).[426]

American Racism: An Idol of Nazi Germany

The Nazis—the political group under Adolf Hitler that murdered millions of Jewish people and others in the Holocaust during World War II—looked to the U.S. for inspiration. Yale Professor James Whitman revealed, "Nazi lawyers looked to American [law] on how to institutionalize racism. ... Some even traveled to the United

States to study in law schools." Interested in voter suppression, the Nazis made maps outlining where Black people's voting rights were restricted and where laws criminalized interracial relationships.

IN MANDELA'S OWN WORDS

When studying history, we often lack the benefit of reading the words of those who've made history. Thankfully, however, the study of modern history provides us such access. Like with King's words and beliefs, Mandela's story and philosophy have undergone attempts of whitewashing, or covering up, inconvenient truths. Yet we have Mandela's autobiography so that Mandela may speak for himself. In it, he speaks of an awareness that many people of African descent in the United States have shared about their own lives:

> During my lifetime, I have dedicated myself to this struggle of the African. I have cherished the ideal of a democratic and free society in which sons live together in harmony with equal opportunities. This then is what the ANC is fighting for. Their struggle is a truly national one. It is a struggle of the African people, inspired by their own suffering and their own experience. It is a struggle for the right to live...[427] A freedom fighter learns the hard way that it is the oppressor who defines the nature of the struggle, and the oppressed is often left no recourse but to use methods that mirror those of the oppressor. At a certain point, one can only fight fire with fire.[428]

Fighting fire wasn't born from a place of hate but rather from the human need to decolonize both the oppressed and oppressor for the evil that displayed itself in different ways:

> It was during those long and lonely years that my hunger for the freedom of my own people became a hunger for the freedom of all people, white and Black. Well as I know anything that the oppressor must be liberated just as surely as the oppressed. A man who takes away another man's freedom is a prisoner... The oppressed and the oppressor robbed of their humanity.[429]

MANDELA AND THE U.S. TERRORIST WATCH LIST

For his activism as a member of the ANC, Mandela was sent to prison in 1962, charged with starting worker strikes and leaving the country without permission. He was given a life sentence, but international pressure for his release eventually forced the apartheid government to let him go. Mandela was released from prison in 1990 and elected president of South Africa in 1994, but he remained on the U.S. terrorist watch list until 2008, at the age of 90.

The reason for remaining on this list was that Mandela was a member (and chairman) of the ANC, and the ANC was added to the list by the administration of President Ronald Reagan at the request of the South African apartheid government that supported the Cold War efforts of the United States. (See "What Will the Neighbors Think?" on page 131 for more on the Cold War.) The South African government worked closely with the administrations of President Richard Nixon and Reagan to limit Soviet and Communist influence in South Africa.

The ANC, however, had participants who were members of the South African Communist Party.[430] The ANC was the only group labeled as a terrorist group by the United States on the entire continent of Africa shortly before Mandela's release from prison. The U.S. government referred to Mandela as a "[terrorist] leader of the ANC," even when he was still in prison.[431]

Mandela remained on that list because he was still a member of the ANC after his release and because of his friendships with world leaders who were considered enemies of the United States. On a trip to the U.S. in 1990, Mandela took part in a town hall meeting in New York City. There, Mandela affirmed his support for leaders like Muammar al-Qaddafi of Libya, Yasser Arafat of the Palestinian Liberation Organization, and Fidel Castro of Cuba, who were all considered terrorist leaders by the United States. When asked why he supported these men, Mandela answered as follows:

Yasser Arafat, Colonel al-Qaddafi, Fidel Castro support our struggle to the hilt.... One of the mistakes that the outside world

RESISTANCE STORIES *from* BLACK HISTORY *for* KIDS

makes is to think that their enemies should be our enemies. ... Our attitude toward any country is determined by the attitude of that country toward our struggle.[432]

When warned about how his comments would be received by others in the U.S, namely the Jewish community and the U.S. Congress, Mandela responded by saying that the ANC "sympathizes with the struggle of the Jewish people down the years. ... That does not mean that the enemies of Israel are our enemies. Anyone who changes his principles, depending on who he is dealing with, is not a man who can lead a nation."[433]

Mandela would not abandon his friends and continued to call out U.S. foreign policy; he pointed out that the U.S. approach to world affairs included doing the same types of activities it accused Mandela's political friends of participating in. It wasn't until 2008 that Mandela was removed from the list when the matter, according to then-Secretary of State Condoleezza Rice, became embarrassing.[434]

CHAPTER 39

WHY WE DAP

I've heard it said that a handshake is revealing; a firm handshake can tell you about a person's integrity, sincerity, and honesty. A handshake, in some cases, is binding, a symbol of an agreement between two people or two groups of people. I think there is some truth to that. But one thing that a handshake is not is intimate. A handshake is a formal greeting among different parties. It's a formal greeting of business. But dap is something different.

WHAT IS DAP?

Dap is an intimate acknowledgment of friends you call family. Dap is communal. Dap is revolutionary. Dap is governance; it symbolizes who we (Black people) are to each other. To give dap is to show love. You may be wondering, what is giving dap? Dap is a specific type of handshake created (and creatively inventive) by Black people. To give dap is when two individuals greet by clasping their right hands but loosely enough so their hands slide into a locking of the fingers.

Dap can be accompanied by a covering of the locked hands with the available hands of the participants, or it may be accompanied by a shoulder to shoulder embrace (with or without a hugging motion by the available arms and hands of the participants). But dap or giving dap (among Black folks) is more than just a greeting. The greeting originated with a purpose. Historically, the dap is both a symbol among African American men that expresses unity, strength, defiance, or resistance and a complex language for communicating information.[435] But dapping is rooted in racial solidarity (unity) that literally saved lives—Black lives to be exact.[436]

HOW DAP CAME TO BE

The practice of dapping originated in the late 1960s among Black soldiers during the Vietnam War as a way to protect each other from racist violence after a Black soldier was murdered by a white soldier and others were shot by white soldiers during combat.[437] Scholars on the Vietnam War and Black Vietnam vets alike note that the dap derived from a promise Black soldiers made to convey their commitment to looking after one another.[438] However, the military outlawed dapping out of fear that dap was code for Black insurrection.[439]

It was rarely used on military posts in the United States, and when it was, it was usually introduced by a soldier who had served overseas.[440] (A GI is a soldier. GI stands for "galvanized Iron.") It has been estimated that hundreds of Black soldiers[441] stationed overseas between 1962 and 1975 were punished by the military for dapping.

Punishments for dapping ranged from an extra duty to spending time in a military prison or getting kicked out the military; nevertheless, the dap flourished among Blacks in the military as a symbol of solidarity and survival.[442] The movements of the dap, an acronym for "dignity and pride," translate to "I'm not above you, you're not above me, we're side by side, we're together." It served as a substitute for the Black power salute prohibited by the military.[443] It even served as a trust builder between Blacks and whites in the military—between recuperating Black soldiers and white medical staff, for example— and was a tool used to root out Black spies.[444]

A PERSONAL WORD ON THE DAP

The great intellectual Ta-Nehisi Coates called giving dap a sacred art. It's because, I believe, there is a right and a wrong way to giving dap. The wrong way will have you slapping a fist because your coordination is off. But when it's right, it is an imperfectly perfect union of individual styles that meet at the intersection of two interpretations of culture; specifically, Black culture when involving two Black people. More than anything, it's an acknowledgment among Black people—among Black men, particularly—that says, "I see you even if the world doesn't; I'm with you and I got you."

I was introduced to the sacred art when watching my father arriving at the door of my grandmother's house to take me home. I was elementary school young. He walked up with my uncle, and prior to them reaching the door, they gave dap. I'm sure they had done this countless times before, but this was the first time I noticed it.

I wondered to myself, What the hell was that and how did they do it? As I got older, I practiced on myself in the mirror. I realized quickly that my left and right hands didn't share good dap chemistry. Yet I attempted to dap just as they did; hands aimed northwest with an open hand clasping, connecting into a crispy finger snap. It was old school. I was a youngblood (as the elders said). They had years of practice. But when I first gave dap at the local park in East Camden, it was natural, instinctive, and crispy.

The ancestors guided my open hand toward my friend's hand on an angle traveling southwest, and our hands connected and clasped, transitioning smoothly into a nice nine-year-old snap. The first time my dad and I gave dap, it felt so damn good. I felt like I finally arrived. It was as though I gained his approval to take my dap international. As a teenager, I honed my dap game through much practice, and by college, my dap game was strong. Now, I can sense different dap on the fly and adjust to produce a perfectly performed dap.

A FINAL WORD

Again, dap is communal; it's governance. It's our intimate greeting and parting. Among family and friends, dap is followed with an embrace because dap shows love in a world that never loved us, a world that has never fully acknowledged Black humanity. Now, I am the old head teaching my son and daughters about the sacred art, and each time, they are perfectly imperfect. It's more than just a greeting with them.

It's my opportunity to funnel the spirit of resistance and humanity shared through this text with them in every dap I give them. It may seem like you can't get that out of a hand-gesturing greeting. But again, it's a sacred art born from a place of protection, solidarity, and an acknowledgment of Black humanity. With every dap I give them, mangled or not, I tell my children what the soldiers told each other: I see you even if the world doesn't; I'm with you and I got you. I hope the ancestors approve.

BY THE NUMBERS: HISTORY OF REPARATION PAYMENTS TO AFRICAN AMERICANS BY THE UNITED STATES*

$10 MILLION

Out-of-court settlement for Tuskegee Experiment victims

$2.1 MILLION

Paid to survivors of the 1923 Rosewood Massacre

$1.2 BILLION

Free Blacks who owned slaves by 1830

$5,500

Money Virginia gave to residents denied an education due to closed schools

$5 MILLION

Money JPMorgan Chase gave to Black students due to its ties to slavery

$10 MILLION

North Carolina payment made to survivors of state eugenics program

$1.7 MILLION

Money Virginia Theological Seminary paid to descendants enslaved

$10 MILLION

Tax dollars set aside by City Council of Evanston, Illnois, for reparations

$27 MILLION

Princeton University payment to initiatives due to its ties to enslavement

* Allen J. Davis, "An Historical Timeline of Reparations Payments Made from 1783 through 2022 by the United States Government, States, Cities, Religious Institutions, Universities, Corporations, and Communities," UMass Amherst Libraries, last updated June 28, 2022, https://guides.library.umass.edu /reparations.

GLOSSARY

abolish: to end

abolition: the action of officially ending something

acknowledge/acknowledgment: to identify as genuine or valid

administration: the act or process of managing or completing something

advantage/take advantage (noun and verb): to have or make good use of something

African Diaspora: communities of people outside of the African continent descended from Africans

agitator: an individual who creates conflict about an issue or person

alliance: a bond or connection between individuals, groups, or governments

Amazigh: an ethic group indigenous to North Africa

American Revolution/Revolutionary War: the war of thirteen settler colonies for independence from Great Britain fought from 1775 to 1783

ancestor: a person who lived many years before people descended from them (for example, a great-grandfather is an ancestor)

antebellum: existing before the Civil War

BCE: before common era (used in place of BC)

capitalist/capitalism: an economic system characterized by private ownership of goods and service labor with the cost determined by free-market competition

captor: someone who has captured a person or a thing

captive: someone captured by a person or a thing

categorize: to separate items, people, or places into specific groupings

CE: common era (used in place of AD)

civil rights: the rights of citizens to be politically, socially, economically, and culturally free

civil rights movement: a movement for racial equality in the U.S. between the 1950s and 1960s

civil war: a war between opposing groups of citizens within a country

communist/communism: a system in which goods are owned by the state and are made or offered to all people as needed

Confederate: a citizen of the former Confederate States of America (the Southern states)

confrontation: a clash of forces or ideas

Congress (U.S.): the top lawmaking group in the United States

conquest: taking someone or something by force

conspiracy: an agreement or action between people to do something illegal or immoral

context: the parts of a conversation that surround a word or passage that explains its meaning

contraception: the purposeful prevention for getting pregnant

defiance: the act of disobeying

democracy/democratic: a government or rule by the people

descendant: proceeding from an ancestor

Diaspora: people who live outside ancestral lands

dominate/domination: to rule or control someone

dynastic/dynasty: a group or family that keeps holds on to power for a long time

economic: relating to consumer goods and services, their production, and consumption

emancipate: to free from the control or the power of another person

Emancipation Proclamation: document that declared all enslaved persons in Confederate territories to be free

RESISTANCE STORIES *from* BLACK HISTORY *for* KIDS

execute: to complete something

exploit: to take advantage of another's work, efforts, needs, or wants

facility: a building or system created to serve a specific purpose, like an office

fugitive: someone who has escaped captivity

Greater Antilles: a large group of islands in the Caribbean, including Cuba, Hispaniola, Jamaica, and Puerto Rico

guerrilla warfare: nontraditional military actions (such as harassment and sabotage) done by small and independent military-like units

Hispaniola: an island of the Greater Antilles with two countries within: Haiti (on the west) and the Dominican Republic (on the east)

Imazighen: the plural form of Amazigh

indentured servant: a person forced to work for another person for a scheduled amount of time

Indigenous: someone who is native to the land they live in

institution: an established organization (bank) or system (criminal justice)

insurrection: an act of revolting against authority or government

intellect/intellectual: knowing information as distinguished from feeling a hunch

legacy: something handed down by or received from an ancestor from the past

Lesser Antilles: smaller Caribbean islands that include Virgin, Leeward, and Windward Islands, Trinidad, Barbados, Tobago, and islands in the southern Caribbean north of Venezuela

liberate/liberation: to set for or actively set free

libertador: Spanish word meaning "liberator"

Maroon: a person of African descent who escaped enslavement and lived in community with others like them

marronage: the process of Maroons establishing permanent or semipermanent towns hidden from plantations

massacre: an act of destruction by murdering people

militia: a group of armed people acting like a military unit, usually motivated by political beliefs

mulatto: an offensive term used to identify a biracial (Black and white) person

oppress/oppressor/oppression: to weigh down others by use of power

petition: a written request for change, signed by many people in support of that call

pilgrimage: a voyage to a monument or holy place as a follower

plantation: an agricultural land usually worked by a resident labor force

raid: a sudden invasion of someone's property by law enforcement

rebellion: open, armed, and sometimes successful resistance against an established government

recruit: to obtain the services or labor of a person

refugee: a person who flees their home for a foreign country to escape danger

reparations: the act of making amends or satisfying a wrong or injury—usually in the form of money

republic: a form of government where supreme power resides in a body of citizens entitled to vote and is exercised by those they elect

resistance: the ability to show force in opposition

revolt: to reject loyalty or enslavement by another person or group

segregate/segregation: the separation or isolation of a race, class, or ethnic group by a government that imposes social, political, and economic barriers by other discriminatory means

stereotype: a general mental picture held in common by members of a group made up of prejudiced attitudes

systemic racism: racism in the laws and institutions of a society or organization that benefits one racial group of people over all others

Thirteenth Amendment: an amendment that states that "neither slavery nor involuntary servitude, except as a punishment for crime whereof the party shall have been duly convicted, shall exist within the United States, or any place subject to their jurisdiction"

Transatlantic slave trade: a period where Europeans traded money and resources for African people

Union (proper noun): the northern portion of the United States of America fighting during the Civil War

Western Hemisphere: the half of the Earth that includes North, Central, and South America as well as the Atlantic and Pacific oceans

Whitewash: the intentional withholding of information to hide a guilty person or groups, acts or deeds

white privilege: a set of social and economic advantages that white people have because of being categorized as white within a society known for racial inequality

NOTES

INTRODUCTION

1. John Henrik Clarke, "The Influence of Arthur A. Schomburg on My Concept of Africana Studies," *Phylon (1960-)* 49, no. 1/2 (1992): 4, https://doi.org/10.2307/3132612.

2. Joel Augustus Rogers, *Africa's Gift to America* (New York: Futuro Press, 1961), 33.

3. Colin A. Palmer, "Defining and Studying the Modern African Diaspora," *The Journal of Negro History* 85, no. 1-2 (2000): 28, https://www.journals.uchicago.edu/doi/10 .1086/JNHv85n1-2p27.

CHAPTER 1: WE'RE LOOKING AT THE WORLD UPSIDE DOWN

4. Chancellor Williams, *The Destruction of Black Civilization: Great Issues of Race From 4500 B.C. to 2000 A.D.* (Chicago, IL: Third World Press, 1974).

5. Joanna Walter, "Boston Public Schools Map Switch Aims to Amend 500 Years of Distortion," *The Guardian,* last updated March 23, 2017, https://www.theguardian.com /education/2017/mar/19/boston-public-schoolsworld-map-mercator-peters -projection?utm_source=pocket_mylist.

6. Jeff Desjardins, "Mapped: Visualizing the True Size of Africa," Visual Capitalist, last updated February 19, 2020, https://www.visualcapitalist.com/map-true-size-of-africa.

7. Nick Danforth, "How the North Ended Up on Top of the Map," AlJazeeraAmerica. com, last updated February 16, 2014, http://america.aljazeera.com/opinions/2014/2 /maps-cartographycolonialismnortheurocentricglobe.html.

8. Thomas J. Bassett, "Indigenous Mapmaking in Intertropical Africa," in *The History of Cartography* (Chicago, IL: University of Chicago Press, 1998), 24-48, https://press .uchicago.edu/books/HOC/HOC_V2_B3/HOC_VOLUME2_Book3_chapter3.pdf.

9. Danforth, "How the North Ended Up on Top of the Map."

10. Bassett, "Indigenous Mapmaking," 24.

11. Bassett, "Indigenous Mapmaking," 24.

12. John Henrik Clarke, "Africa in Early World History," *Ebony Magazine* (1976): 125-128.

13. Itibari M. Zulu, "The Ancient Kemetic Roots of Library and Information," *The First National Conference of African American Librarians* (1993): 246-266, https://files.eric .ed.gov/fulltext/ED382204.pdf.

14. Zulu, "The Ancient Kemetic Roots," 246.

CHAPTER 2: THE ANCIENT AFRICAN CIVILIZATIONS MISSING FROM MANY TEXTS

15. John Henrik Clarke, "Ancient Civilizations of Africa: The Missing Pages in World History," *Présence Africaine*, no. 130 (1984), 148-58, https://www.jstor.org/stable /24350947.

16. Bill Hoffman, "Ancient Egypt Had Toothpaste," *New York Post*, last updated January 20, 2003, https://nypost.com/2003/01/20/ancient-egypt-had-toothpaste.

17. Vanessa Davies, "How Egyptologists Removed Ancient Egypt from Africa," Museum of Fine Art Boston, accessed October 5, 2022, https://www.mfa.org /exhibitions/nubia/vanessa-davies.

18. Clarke, "Ancient Civilizations of Africa," 150.

19. Clarke, "Ancient Civilizations of Africa," 149.

20. Gaston Maspero, *The Dawn of Civilization* (NY: Frederick Unger Company, 2010).

21. Clarke, "Africa in Early World History," 126.

22. Flora Louisa Shaw, *A Tropical Dependency: An Outline of the Ancient History of the Western Sudan With an Account of the Settlement of Nigeria* (London: Frank Cass, Ltd., 2017).

23. Ashley Strickland, "How Did Lucy, Our Early Human Ancestor, Die 3 Million Years Ago?" *CNN*, last updated August 30, 2016, https://www.cnn.com/2016/08/29/health /lucy-early-human-ancestor-cause-of-death/index.html.

24. Ayele Bekerie, "Ethiopica: Some Historical Reflections on the Origin of the Word Ethiopia," *International Journal of Ethiopian Studies* 1, no. 2 (2004), 110-21, https://www .jstor.org/stable/27828841.

25. Bekerie, "Ethiopia," 115.

26. Boyce Rensberger, "Ancient Nubian Artifacts Yield Evidence of Earliest Monarchy," *The New York Times*, March 1, 1979, https://www.nytimes.com/1979/03/01/archives /ancient-nubian-artifacts-yield-evidence-ofearliest-monarchy-clues.html.

27. Clarke, "Africa in Early World History," 126-127.

28. Clarke, "Africa in Early World History," 127.

29. Rensberger, "Ancient Nubian Artifacts."

30. National Geographic, "The Kingdom of Aksum," *National Geographic*, accessed September 17, 2022, https://www.nationalgeographic.org/article/kingdom-aksum/12th -grade.

31. National Geographic, "The Kingdom of Aksum."

32. Clarke, "Africa in Early World History," 127.

33. Clarke, "Africa in Early World History," 127.

34. Clarke, "Africa in Early World History," 127.

35. National Geographic, "The Mali Empire," *National Geographic*, April 26, 2022, https://www.nationalgeographic.org/encyclopedia/mali-empire.

36. National Geographic, "The Mali Empire."

37. Clarke, "Africa in Early World History," 127.

38. Clarke, "Africa in Early World History," 127.

39. Clarke, "Africa in Early World History," 127.

40. Clarke, "Africa in Early World History," 127.

CHAPTER 3: THE RICHEST MAN IN HISTORY

41. "Mansa" is a title meaning emperor.

42. "Mansa Musa Net Worth," CelebrityNetWorth.com, accessed October 5, 2022, https://www.celebritynetworth.com/richest-politicians/royals/mansa-musa-net -worth.

43. Davic C. Conrad, *Empires of Medieval West Africa: Ghana, Mali, and Songhay* (New York: Chelsea House Publications, 2009).

44. Conrad, *Empires of Medieval West Africa*, 46.

45. Naima Mohamud, "Is Mansa Musa the Richest Man Who Ever Lived?" *BBC*, March 10, 2019, https://www.bbc.com/news/world-africa-47379458.

46. Mohamud, "Is Mansa Musa the Richest Man Who Ever Lived?"

47. Clarke, "Africa in Early World History," 127.

48. Jason Daley, "New Exhibition Highlights Story of the Richest Man Who Ever Lived," *Smithsonian Magazine*, last updated February 5, 2019, https://www.smithsonianmag.com/smart-news/richest-man-who-ever-lived-180971409.

49. Clarke, "Africa in Early World History," 127.

50. Conrad, *Great Empires of the Past*, 47.

51. Daley, "New Exhibition Highlights Story of the Richest Man Who Ever Lived."

52. Steve Johnson, "The Richest Man Ever Was Not Named Gates or Bezos; He Was King of Mali in the Middle Ages," *Chicago Tribune*, last updated January 27, 2019, https://www.chicagotribune.com/entertainment/museums/ct-ent-caravans-of-gold-block-museum-0124-story.html.

53. Clarke, "Africa in Early World History," 127.

54. National Geographic, "Mansa Musa (Musa I of Mali)," *National Geographic*, April 27, 2022, https://www.nationalgeographic.org/encyclopedia/mansa-musa-musa-i-mali.

CHAPTER 4: A CHOSEN LAND AND A CHOSEN PEOPLE

55. John Henrik Clarke, "Balancing History," *Black World* (1973): 12–25.

56. Clarke, "Balancing History," 15.

57. John Henrik Clarke, "The Black Woman in World History: On the Cultural Unity of Africa," *Black World*, 24, no. 4 (1975): 12–26.

58. Clarke, "Balancing History," 14.

59. Clarke, "Balancing History," 14.

60. Clarke, "The Black Woman in World History," 22.

61. Clarke, "Balancing History," 16.

62. Clarke, "Balancing History," 15.

63. Clarke, "Balancing History," 15.

CHAPTER 5: THEY CAME BEFORE COLUMBUS

64. Dennis W. Zotigh and Renee Gokey, "Rethinking How We Celebrate American History—Indigenous Peoples' Day," *Smithsonian Magazine*, last updated October 12, 2020, https://www.smithsonianmag.com/blogs/national-museum-american-indian/2020/10/12/indigenous-peoples-day-updated2020.

65. Ivan Van Sertima, *They Came Before Columbus: The African Presence in Ancient America* (NY: Random House, 1976).

66. Van Sertima, *They Came Before Columbus*, a8.

67. John Henrik Clarke, "The Impact of the African on the New World: A Reappraisal," *Presence Africaine*, no. 79, (1971): 3–16.

68. Van Sertima, *They Came Before Columbus*, 13.

69. Van Sertima, *They Came Before Columbus*, 13.

70. Van Sertima, *They Came Before Columbus*, 14.

71. Van Sertima, *They Came Before Columbus*, 15.

72. Van Sertima, *They Came Before Columbus*, 16.

73. Clarke, "The Impact of the African on the New World," 33.

74. Clarke, "The Impact of the African on the New World," 33.
75. Clarke, "The Impact of the African on the New World," 33.
76. Clarke, "The Impact of the African on the New World," 32.
77. Clarke, "The Impact of the African on the New World," 33.
78. Rogers, *Africa's Gift to America*, 17.
79. Clarke, "The Impact of the African on the New World," 33.
80. Clarke, "The Impact of the African on the New World," 33.
81. Clarke, "The Impact of the African on the New World," 32.
82. Clarke, "The Impact of the African on the New World," 32.

CHAPTER 6: THE QUEEN CALLED KING

83. Clarke, "The Black Woman in History," 22.
84. Clarke, "The Black Woman in History," 22.
85. Joel Augustus Rogers, *World's Great Men of Color*, Volume 2 (New York: Macmillan, 1947).
86. Clarke, "The Black Woman in History," 23.
87. Clarke, "The Black Woman in History," 23.
88. Clarke, "The Black Woman in History," 23.
89. Clarke, "The Black Woman in History," 23–24.
90. Rogers, *World's Great Men of Color*, 249.
91. Clarke, "The Black Woman in History," 24.
92. Clarke, "The Black Woman in History," 24.

CHAPTER 7: THE QUEEN CALLED KING

93. Rogers, *Africa's Gift to America*, 38.
94. Rogers, *Africa's Gift to America*, 35.
95. This partially replaced the previous triangular trade; Europe, Africa, and the New World.
96. Rogers, *Africa's Gift to America*, 43.
97. Rogers, *Africa's Gift to America*, 43.
98. Rogers, *Africa's Gift to America*, 43.
99. Alfred Blumrosen and Ruth Blumrosen, *Slave Nation: How Slavery United the Colonies and Sparked the American Revolution* (Naperville, IL: Sourcebooks, Inc., 2006), 1–2.
100. Blumrosen and Blumrosen, *Slave Nation*, 11.
101. Blumrosen and Blumrosen, *Slave Nation*, 30.

CHAPTER 8: L'OUVERTURE AND THE TAKING OF SAINT-DOMINGUE

102. Rann Miller, "We've Never Forgiven Haiti for Being Black," *The Progressive*, October 1, 2019, https://progressive.org/latest/forgive-haiti-for-being-black-miller-191001.
103. Russell L. Adams, *Great Negroes Past and Present*, third edition (Chicago, IL: Afro-American Publishing Company, 1969), 16–19.
104. John Henrik Clarke, "Toussaint-Louverture and the Haitian Revolution," *Présence Africaine*, no. 89 (1974): 179–87, https://www.jstor.org/stable/24349711.
105. Rogers, *World's Great Men of Color*, 228.
106. Clarke, "Balancing History," 23.

107. Clarke, "Balancing History," 23.

108. Rogers, *World's Great Men of Color*, 232.

109. Rogers, *World's Great Men of Color*, 233.

110. Rogers, *World's Great Men of Color*, 233.

111. Miller, "We've Never Forgiven Haiti for Being Black."

112. Robert M. Poole, "What Became of the Taíno?" *Smithsonian Magazine*, October 2011, https://www.smithsonianmag.com/travel/what-became-of-the-taino-73824867.

113. Edward E. Baptist, "The Bittersweet Victory at Saint-Domingue," *Slate*, last updated August 6, 2015, https://slate.com/human-interest/2015/08/the-most -successful-slave-rebellion-in-history-created-an-independent-haiti-and-secured -the-louisiana-purchase-and-the-expansion-of-north-american-slavery.html.

114. Miller, "We've Never Forgiven Haiti for Being Black."

115. Rogers, *World's Great Men of Color*, 243.

116. Miller, "We've Never Forgiven Haiti for Being Black."

CHAPTER 9: THE GREAT ESCAPE OF ONA JUDGE

117. Mt. Vernon Ladies Association, "10 Facts About Washington & Slavery," MountVernon.org, accessed March 18, 2022, George Washington's Mount Vernon: https://www.mountvernon.org/george-washington/slavery/ten-facts-about -washington-slavery.

118. Erica A. Dunbar, *Never Caught: The Washingtons' Relentless Pursuit of Their Runaway Slave, Ona Judge* (NY: 37 INK, 2017).

119. Dunbar, *Never Caught*, 13.

120. Cassie Owens, "Pennsylvania Officially Abolished Slavery in 1780. But Many Black Pennsylvanians Were in Bondage Long After That," *Philadelphia Inquirer*, February 27, 2019, https://www.inquirer.com/news/blackhistory-month-pennsylvania-gradual -abolition-slavery-indentureemancipation-20190227.html.

121. Dunbar, *Never Caught*, 69, 80.

122. Michele L. Norris, "George and Martha Washington Enslaved 300 People. Let's Start with Their Names," *The Washington Post*, June 26, 2020, https://www .washingtonpost.com/opinions/george-and-martha-washington-enslaved-300 -people-lets-start-with-theirnames/2020/06/26/d3f7c362-b7e7-11ea-a510 -55bf26485c93_story.html.

123. Norris, "George and Martha Washington Enslaved 300 People," 67.

124. Norris, "George and Martha Washington Enslaved 300 People," 77–78.

125. Dunbar, *Never Caught*, 110.

126. Dunbar, *Never Caught*, 112.

127. Erica A. Dunbar, "George Washington, Slave Catcher," *The New York Times*, last updated February 16, 2015, https://www.nytimes.com/2015/02/16/opinion/george -washington-slave-catcher.html.

128. Dunbar, "George Washington, Slave Catcher."

CHAPTER 10: HAITI AND EL LIBERTADOR'S GREAT BETRAYAL

129. Gerarld Horne, "The Haitian Revolution and the Central Question of African American History," *The Journal of African American History* 100, no. 1 (2015): 26–58, https://www.journals.uchicago.edu/doi/abs/10.5323/jafriamerhist.100.1.0026 ?journalCode=jaah.

130. Horne, "The Haitian Revolution and African American History," 30.
131. "Defining Diaspora," DePaul.edu, accessed October 5, 2022, https://las.depaul
.edu/centers-and-institutes/center-for-black-diaspora/about/Pages/defining
-diaspora.aspx.
132. Palmer, "Defining and Studying the Modern African Diaspora," 28.
133. Horne, "The Haitian Revolution and African American History," 30.
134. Horne, "The Haitian Revolution and African American History," 38–39.
135. Horne, "The Haitian Revolution and African American History," 40.
136. Horne, "The Haitian Revolution and African American History," 42.
137. Horne, "The Haitian Revolution and African American History," 41.
138. Horne, "The Haitian Revolution and African American History," 39.
139. France Francois, "Haiti Aided Latin American Independence Movements; Latinxs
Are Returning the Favor with Silence & Broken Promises," *Refinery 29*, last updated
October 7, 2021, https://www.refinery29.com/en-us/2021/10/10688116/haiti-latin
-american-independence-essay.
140. Mohammed Elnaiem, "Bolivar in Haiti," *JStor Daily*, last updated December 24,
2019, https://daily.jstor.org/bolivar-haiti.
141. Elnaiem, "Bolivar in Haiti."
142. Elnaiem, "Bolivar in Haiti."
143. Francois, "Haiti Aided Latin American Independence Movements."
144. Horne, "The Haitian Revolution and African American History," 43.
145. Francois, "Haiti Aided Latin American Independence Movements."
146. Francois, "Haiti Aided Latin American Independence Movements."

CHAPTER 11: THE FIRST BLACK PRESIDENT

147. Alice L. Baumgartner, *South to Freedom: Runaway Slaves to Mexico and the
Road to the Civil War* (New York: Hachette Book Group, 2020).
148. Baumgartner, *South to Freedom*, 64.
149. William Loren Katz, "The Legacy of Vicente Guerrero: Mexico's First Black Indian
President," University of Florida Press, 2001, https://web.archive.org/web/20160809211623
/http://williamlkatz.com/legacy-of-vicente-guerrero.
150. Patricia Ann Talley and Candelaria Donaji Mendez Tello, "Research Reveals
the African-Indigenous Heritage of Mexican President Vicente Guerrero," accessed
March 10, 2022, https://static1.squarespace.com/static/57b74931b3db2be1cef4e3c8
/t/588fa13b6b8f5bb9cf2f50e6/1485807933414/ResearchRevealstheAfrican
-IndigenousHeritageofMexicanPresidentVicenteGuerrero.pdf.
151. Theodore G. Vincent, "The Contributions of Mexico's First Black Indian President,
Vicente Guerrero," *The Journal of Negro History* 86, no. 2 (2001): 148–159, https://
www.journals.uchicago.edu/doi/10.2307/1350162.
152. Vincent, "The Contributions of Vicente Guerrero," 151–152.
153. Vincent, "The Contributions of Vicente Guerrero," 152.
154. Baumgartner, *South to Freedom*, 67.
155. Baumgartner, *South to Freedom*, 67.
156. Paul Ortiz, *An African American and Latinx History of the United States* (Boston,
MA: Beacon Press, 2018), 40.
157. Ortiz, *An African American and Latinx History of the United States*, 40.
158. Vincent, "The Contributions of Vicente Guerrero," 153.
159. Vincent, "The Contributions of Vicente Guerrero," 153.

CHAPTER 12: FREDERICK DOUGLASS: WRESTLING WITH THE MASTER

160. David W. Blight, *Frederick Douglass: Prophet of Freedom* (New York: Simon & Schuster, 2018).

161. Blight, *Frederick Douglass*.

162. Federick Douglass, *Narrative of the Life of Frederick Douglass: An American Slave*, 1845, 33.

163. Douglass, *Narrative of the Life of Frederick Douglass*, 38.

164. Douglass, *Narrative of the Life of Frederick Douglass*, 38.

CHAPTER 13: THE AFRICAN ALLIANCE THAT ALMOST WAS

165. Vincent, "The Contributions of Vicente Guerrero," 149.

166. Baumgartner, *South to Freedom*, 69.

167. Baumgartner, *South to Freedom*, 69.

168. Baumgartner, *South to Freedom*, 71.

169. Baumgartner, *South to Freedom*, 74.

CHAPTER 14: MAROON COMMUNITIES IN THE UNITED STATES

170. Henry Louis Gates Jr., *100 Amazing Facts About the Negro* (NY: Pantheon Books, 2017).

171. Gates, *100 Amazing Facts About the Negro*.

172. Herbert Aptheker, "Maroons Within the Present Limits of the United States," *The Journal of Negro* 24, no. 2 (1939): 167–184, www.journals.uchicago.edu/doi/10.2307 /2714447.

173. Daniel O. Sayers, P. Brendan Burke, and Aaron M. Henry, "The Political Economy of Exile in the Great Dismal Swamp," *International Journal of Historical Archaeology* 11, no. 1 (2007): 60–97, https://www.jstor.org/stable/20853121.

174. Sayers et al., "The Political Economy of Exile," 71.

175. Sayers et al., "The Political Economy of Exile," 168.

176. "Maroon Community," *Encyclopedia Britannica*, accessed May 5, 2022, https://www.britannica.com/topic/maroon-community."

177. "Maroon Community," *Encyclopedia Britannica*.

178. Samuel A. Cartwright, "Diseases and Peculiarities of the Negro Race," *Southern & Western States XI (1851)*, https://www.pbs.org/wgbh/aia/part4/4h3106t.html.

179. Sayers et al., "The Political Economy of Exile," 60.

180. Sayers et al., "The Political Economy of Exile," 60.

181. Sayers et al., "The Political Economy of Exile," 73.

182. James Redpath, *The Roving Editors, or, Talks with Slaves in Southern States* (New York: A. B. Burdick, 1859).

183. Sayers et al., "The Political Economy of Exile," 74–75.

CHAPTER 15: MAROON COMMUNITIES IN THE AFRICAN DIASPORA

184. "Maroon Community," *Encyclopedia Britannica*.

185. "Maroon History," Harvard.edu, accessed October 5, 2022, https://cyber.harvard .edu/eon/maroon/history.html.

186. "Maroon History," Harvard.edu.

187. National Library of Jamaica, "The Jamaican Maroons," National Library of Jamaica, accessed September 26, 2022, https://nlj.gov.jm/history-notes/The%20 Maroons%20edited%20final.html.
188. Ashante Infantry, "Meet the Legendary Community That Fought for Its Freedom in Jamaica," *National Geographic*, last updated February 19, 2021, https://www .nationalgeographic.com/travel/article/legendary-community-that-fought-for-its -freedom-in-Jamaica.
189. Infantry, "Meet the Legendary Community,"
190. Infantry, "Meet the Legendary Community,"
191. Infantry, "Meet the Legendary Community."
192. Robert Nelson Anderson, "The Quilombo of Palmares: A New Overview of a Maroon State in Seventeenth-Century Brazil," *Journal of Latin American Studies* 28, no. 3 (1996): 545-566, www.jstor.org/stable/157694.
193. Mohammed Elnaiem, "Black Conquistadors and Black Maroons," *JStor Daily*, last updated April 1, 2021, https://daily.jstor.org/ black-conquistadors-and-black-maroons.
194. Elnaiem, "Black Conquistadors and Black Maroons."
195. Elnaiem, "Black Conquistadors and Black Maroons."
196. Anderson, "The Quilombo of Palmares," 563.
197. Anderson, "The Quilombo of Palmares," 563.
198. Anderson, "The Quilombo of Palmares," 563.
199. Matthew Wills, "Brazil's Maroon State," *JStor Daily*, last updated July 11, 2019, https://daily.jstor.org/brazils-maroon-state.
200. Wills, "Brazil's Maroon State."

CHAPTER 16: NO NEW BABIES

201. Liese M. Perrin, "Resisting Reproduction: Reconsidering Slave Contraception in the Old South," *Journal of American Studies* 35, no. 2 (2001): 255-274.
202. Soujouner Truth, "Ain't I A Woman?" Delivered May 29, 1851, Akron, Ohio, https:// thehermitage.com/wp-content/uploads/2016/02/SojournerTruth_Aint-I-a-Woman _1851.pdf."
203. Perrin, "Resisting Reproduction," 257.
204. Antebellum means before the Civil War. The Antebellum period, where enslavement was the law of the land, was in effect at the formal start of the United States until the Civil War.
205. Perrin, "Resisting Reproduction," 260.
206. Perrin, "Resisting Reproduction," 259.
207. Perrin, "Resisting Reproduction," 258.
208. Perrin, "Resisting Reproduction," 258.
209. Perrin, "Resisting Reproduction," 258-259.

CHAPTER 17: REVOLTS OF THE ENSLAVED IN THE UNITED STATES

210. Western societies are those located in Europe, North America, Central America, South America, and the Caribbean.
211. According to historian Herbert Aptheker, enslaved African people's resistance against their enslavement took eight forms: purchasing freedom; strikes; sabotage; suicide and self-mutilation; flight (running away); enlisting in the armed forces; anti-enslavement agitation in speaking and writing; and revolts. Revolts were a result

of three factors: economic hardship; unusual excitement about enslavement, that is, some kind of war; and large additions to the enslaved population.

212. According a Southern Poverty Law Center report, *Teaching Hard History*, American public–school students have a distorted if not severely incomplete understanding of enslavement, its impact on America's economic history, and resistance to it by enslaved Black people. Students are aware of only so much about enslavement.

213. Herbert Aptheker, "American Negro Slave Revolts," *Science & Society* 1, no. 4 (1937): 512–538, www.jstor.org/stable/40399115.

214. Article 1, Section 8, Clause 15 of the U.S. Constitution states that Congress has the power "provide for calling forth the Militia to execute the Laws of the Union, suppress Insurrections and repel Invasions."

215. For a more exhaustive text, refer to Herbert Aptheker's "American Negro Slave Revolts."

CHAPTER 18: REVOLTS OF THE ENSLAVED THROUGHOUT THE DIASPORA

216. Ortiz, *An African American and Latinx History of the United States*.

217. According to University of Wisconsin Professor Michael P. Gueno, the name "Taino" came into common usage in the twentieth century and "Taino" was assigned by historians and anthropologist to refer to the entire Indigenous population of western Caribbean peoples; the correct names for the Indigenous people of this region are the Arawak of the Greater Antilles and the Carib of the Lower Antilles.

CHAPTER 19: WHITE WARS AND BLACK LIVES

218. Junius P. Rodriguez, *Encyclopedia of Slave Resistance and Rebellion*, Volume 1: A–N (Westport, CT: Greenwood Press, 2006).

219. Rogers, *Africa's Gift to America*, 103.

220. Rogers, *Africa's Gift to America*, 103.

221. Rogers, *Africa's Gift to America*, 103.

222. Rodriguez, *Encyclopedia of Slave Resistance and Rebellion*, 62–63.

223. Rodriguez, *Encyclopedia of Slave Resistance and Rebellion*, 63.

224. Jonathan D. Sutherland, *African Americans at War*, Volume 1 (Santa Barbara, CA: ABC-CLIO, 2003).

225. Sutherland, *African Americans at War*, 153.

226. Sutherland, *African Americans at War*, 153.

227. Rodriguez, *Encyclopedia of Slave Resistance and Rebellion*, 65.

CHAPTER 20: THE SEMINOLE WARS AND THE LEGEND OF JOHN HORSE

228. Patrick Pinak, "Why Florida State Can Keep Using Chief Osceola & Renegade as Symbols," *Fanbuzz*, September 16, 2022, https://fanbuzz.com/college-football/acc /florida-state/florida-state-mascot.

229. Pinak, "Why Florida State Can Keep."

230. Pinak, "Why Florida State Can Keep."

231. Francis X. Clines, "Reagan's Doubts on Dr. King Disclosed," *The New York Times*, October 22, 1983, https://www.nytimes.com/1983/10/22/us/reagan-s-doubts-on-dr -king-disclosed.html.

232. Anthony E. Dixon, "Black Seminole Ethnogenisis: Origins, Cultural Characteristics, and Alliances," *Phylon* 57, no. 1 (2020): 8–24, https://www.jstor.org/stable/26924984.

233. Dixon, "Black Seminole Ethnogenisis," 14.

234. Dixon, "Black Seminole Ethnogenisis," 15.

235. Kenneth W. Porter, "Negroes and the Seminole War, 1817–1818," *The Journal of Negro History* 36, no. 3 (1951): 249–280, https://www.jstor.org/stable/2715671.

236. Porter, "Negroes and the Seminole War, 1817–1818," 253.

237. Porter, "Negroes and the Seminole War, 1817–1818," 271.

238. Phillip Thomas Tucker, "John Horse: Forgotten African–American Leader of the Second Seminole War," *The Journal of Negro History* 77, (1992): 74–83, https://www.journals.uchicago.edu/doi/abs/10.2307/3031484?journalCode=jnh.

239. Tucker, "John Horse: Forgotten African–American Leader," 75.

240. Tucker, "John Horse: Forgotten African–American Leader."

241. Tucker, "John Horse: Forgotten African–American Leader, 77.

242. Tucker, "John Horse: Forgotten African–American Leader,"

243. Tucker, "John Horse: Forgotten African–American Leader."

244. Tucker, "John Horse: Forgotten African–American Leader," 81.

245. Tucker, "John Horse: Forgotten African–American Leader."

246. Tucker, "John Horse: Forgotten African–American Leader."

247. Tucker, "John Horse: Forgotten African–American Leader," 82.

248. Porter, "Negroes and the Seminole War, 1835–1842," 427.

249. Porter, "Negroes and the Seminole War, 1817–1818," 427.

CHAPTER 21: GREAT ESCAPES DURING THE ANTEBELLUM

250. The term "antebellum" means before the war. The antebellum in the United States is the period of enslavement prior to the Civil War.

251. Sydney Trent, "Slavery Cost Him His Family. That's When Henry 'Box' Brown Mailed Himself to Freedom," *The Washington Post*, last updated December 28 2019, https://www.washingtonpost.com/history/2019/12/28/slavery-cost-him-his-family-thats-when-henry-boxbrown-mailed-himself-freedom.

252. Henry Louis Jr. Gates, "Which Slave Mailed Himself to Freedom? Really!" *The Root*, last updated May 6, 2013, https://www.theroot.com/which-slave-mailed-himself-to-freedom-really-1790896323.

253. Gates, "Which Slave Mailed Himself to Freedom? Really!"

254. Hollis Robbins, "Fugitive Mail: The Deliverance of Henry 'Box' Brown and Antebellum Postal Politics," *American Studies* 50, no. 1 (2009): 5–25, https://www.jstor.org/stable/41057153

255. Robbins, "Fugitive Mail," 20.

256. Gates, *100 Amazing Facts About the Negro*, 107.

257. Gates, *100 Amazing Facts About the Negro*, 108.

258. "Robert Smalls," *Negro History Bulletin* 5, no. 6 (1942): 127, https://www.jstor.org/stable/44246288.

259. "Robert Smalls," 127.

260. "The Thrilling Escape of William and Ellen Craft," *Negro History Bulletin* 1, no. 1 (1937): 1–5, www.jstor.org/stable/442457.

261. "The Thrilling Escape of William and Ellen Craft," 1.

262. "The Thrilling Escape of William and Ellen Craft," 1.

CHAPTER 22: PASSING, ANOTHER KIND OF RESISTANCE

263. Martha J. Cutter, "'As White as Most White Women:' Racial Passing in Advertisements for Runaway Slaves and the Origins of a Multivalent Term," *American Studies* 54, no. 4 (2016): 73-97, DOI: 10.1353/ams.2016.0017.

264. Cutter, "'As White as Most White Women:' Racial Passing in Advertisements for Runaway Slaves and the Origins of a Multivalent Term," 74.

CHAPTER 23: THE DISASTERS OF CHIRIQUI & ÎLE À VACHE

265. Rashida Talib from Michigan, Ilhan Omar from Minnesota, Ayanna Pressley from Massachusetts and Alexandria Ocasio-Cortez from New York.

266. Rann Miller, "On Being Told to 'Go Back.'" The Progressive, July 22, 2019, https://progressive.org/latest/on-being-told-to-go-back-Miller-190722."

267. Miller, "On Being told to 'Go Back.'"

268. Fodei Batty, "How to Understand the Complicated History of 'Go Back to Africa,'" *The Washington Post*, last updated April 26, 2022, www.washingtonpost.com/news/monkey-cage/wp/2016/04/26/is-go-backto-africa-always-an-insult-heres-a-brief-history-of-american-back-toafrica-movements.

269. Douglas R. Egerton, ""Its Origin Is Not a Little Curious:" A New Look at the American Colonization Society," *Rebels, Reformers, and Revolutionaries* (England, UK: Routledge, 2002), 463-480.

270. Gates, *100 Amazing Facts About the Negro*, 380.

271. Kate Masur, "The African American Delegation to Abraham Lincoln: A Reappraisal," *Civil War History* 56, no. 2 (2010): 117-144, DOI: 10.1353/cwh.0.0149.

272. Miller, "On Being Told to 'Go Back.'"

273. Henry Louis Gates Jr., "Did Lincoln Want to Ship Black People Back to Africa?" *The Root*, last updated January 5, 2015, https://www.theroot.com/did-lincoln-want-to-ship-black-people-back-to-africa-1790858389.

274. Gates, "Did Lincoln Want to Ship Black People Back to Africa?"

275. Masur, "The African American Delegation to Abraham Lincoln," 119-120.

276. Masur, "The African American Delegation to Abraham Lincoln," 122.

277. Rick Beard, "Lincoln's Panama Plan," *The New York Times*, last updated August 16, 2022, https://opinionator.blogs.nytimes.com/2012/08/16/lincolns-panama-plan.

278. Masur, "The African American Delegation to Abraham Lincoln," 122.

279. Miller, "On Being Told to 'Go Back.'"

280. Phillip W. Magness, "The Île à Vache: From Hope to Disaster," *The New York Times*, April 12, 2013, https://opinionator.blogs.nytimes.com/2013/04/12/the-le-vache-from-hope-to-disaster."

281. Magness, "The Île à Vache: From Hope to Disaster."

CHAPTER 24: THE BATTLE OF PINE SWAMP AT TIMBUCTOO

282. Giles R. Wright, *Afro-Americans in New Jersey: A Short History* (Trenton, NJ: New Jersey Historical Commission, 1988).

283. Wright, *Afro-Americans in New Jersey*, 36, 38.

284. Wright, *Afro-Americans in New Jersey*, 2.

285. Wright, *Afro-Americans in New Jersey*, 9.

286. Wright, *Afro-Americans in New Jersey*.

287. The U.S. Marshal's Office has a number of functions including organizing fugitive operations and executing federal arrest warrants.

288. Guy Weston, "Battle at Pine Swamp," *Journal of the Afro-American Historical and Genealogical Society* 35 (2018): 30–32, https://www.dropbox.com/s/kajkae8s3dk1j1h.

289. Christopher B. Barton, "Antebellum African-American Settlements in Southern New Jersey," *African Diaspora Archaeology Newsletter* 12, no. 4 (2009): 1–15, https://scholarworks.umass.edu/cgi/viewcontent.cgi?article=1824&context=adan.

CHAPTER 25: HARRIET TUBMAN: THE GREATEST AMERICAN WHO EVER WAS

290. Kate Clifford Larson, "Harriet Ross Tubman: Timeline," *Meridians* 12, no. 2 (2014): 9–27, https://www.jstor.org/stable/10.2979/meridians.12.2.9.

291. Larson, "Harriet Ross Tubman: Timeline," 11.

292. Erica Dunbar, *She Came to Slay: The Life and Times of Harriet Tubman* (NY: 37 INK, 2019).

293. Dunbar, *She Came to Slay*, 31–32.

294. Dunbar, *She Came to Slay*, 34.

295. Larson, "Harriet Ross Tubman: Timeline," 13.

296. Larson, "Harriet Ross Tubman: Timeline," 13.

297. Dunbar, *She Came to Slay*, 50.

298. Dunbar, *She Came to Slay*, 139.

299. Larson, "Harriet Ross Tubman: Timeline," 14.

300. Graham Gao Hodges Russell, *Black New Jersey: 1664 to the Present Day* (New Brunswick, NJ: Rutgers University Press, 2018).

CHAPTER 26: THE REAL INDEPENDENCE DAY

301. Blumrosen et al., *Slave Nation*, 125–126.

302. Blumrosen et al., *Slave Nation*, 125–126.

303. Blumrosen et al., *Slave Nation*, 137–138.

304. Federick Douglass, "The Meaning of July Fourth for the Negro," *PBS: Africans in America*, May 16, 2022, https://www.pbs.org/wgbh/aia/part4/4h2927t.html.

305. W.E.B. DuBois, *Black Reconstruction in America, 1860-1880* (NY: Free Press, 1998).

306. DuBois, *Black Reconstruction in America, 1860-1880*, 57.

307. DuBois, *Black Reconstruction in America, 1860-1880*, a67.

308. Rann Miller, "Teaching Juneteenth in Schools is Crucial Amid Debates About How to Tackle U.S. History," *The Philadelphia Inquirer*, June 10, 2020, https://www.inquirer.com/opinion/commentary/juneteenth-schoolseducation-us-history-20210613.html.

309. Juneteenth.com, accessed May 16, 2022, https://www.juneteenth.com.

310. Rann Miller, "On Juneteenth, Don't Forget Black Texans," *The Progressive*, June 18, 2022, https://progressive.org/latest/on-juneteenth-dont-forget-black-texans-miller-220618.

311. "Private Companies Producing with US Prison Labor in 2020: Prison Labor in the US Part II," CorporateAccountabilityLab.org, accessed October 5, 2022, https://corpaccountabilitylab.org/calblog/2020/8/5/private-companies-producing-with-us-prison-labor-in-2020-prison-labor-in-the-us-part-ii.

312. Miller, "On Juneteenth, Don't Forget Black Texans."

CHAPTER 27: GIVING CREDIT WHERE CREDIT IS DUE

313. Nerisha Penrose, "TikTok Was Built on the Backs of Black Creators. Why Can't They Get Any Credit?" *Elle*, April 29, 2021, https://www.elle.com/culture/a36178170 .black-tiktok-creators-mya-nicole-chris-cotter-addison-rae-jimmy-fallon.

314. Njera Perkins, "The Black TikTok Strike Isn't About Crediting Viral Dances, It's About Protecting Black Creativity In Digital Spaces," *AfroTech*, July 28, 2021, https:// afrotech.com/black-tiktok-strike-protecting-black-creativity-digital-spaces.

315. Distillation is the process of making whiskey by separating alcoholic liquids from fermented items, usually foods items transformed into alcoholic materials.

316. Clay Risen, "When Jack Daniel's Failed to Honor a Slave, an Author Rewrote History," *New York Times*, August 15, 2017, https://www.nytimes.com/2017/08/15/dining /jack-daniels-whiskey-slave-nearest-green.html."

317. Edward S. Jenkins, "Bridging the Two Cultures: American Black Scientists and Inventors," *Journal of Black Studies* 21, no. 3 (1991): 313–324, www.jstor.org/stable /2784340.

318. Jenkins, "Bridging the Two Cultures," 318.

319. Jenkins, "Bridging the Two Cultures," 318.

CHAPTER 28: THE ORIGIN AND PURPOSE OF BLACK HISTORY MONTH

320. Javis R. Givens, *Fugitive Pedagogy: Carter G. Woodson and the Art of Black Teaching* (Cambridge, MA: Harvard University Press, 2021).

321. Carter G. Woodson, "Negro History Week 1934 Brochure," *Folder 36* (1936): 3.

322. Monique Beals, "Alabama Schools Official Reports Complaints of Black History Month As Teaching Critical Race Theory," *The Hill*, last updated February 3, 2022, www.thehill.com/homenews/state-watch/592687-alabama-state-school-official -reports-complaints-of-black-history-month.

323. Carter G. Woodson, "Negro History Week," *The Journal of Negro History* 11, no. 2 (1926): 238–242, https://www.journals.uchicago.edu/doi/10.2307/2714171.

CHAPTER 29: BLACK FREEDOM, WHITE ANGER, AND A RED SUMMER

324. History.com Editors, "Black Leaders During Reconstruction," *History*, last updated August 25, 2022, https://www.history.com/topics/american-civil-war/black -leaders-during-reconstruction.

325. Abigail Higgins, "Red Summer of 1919: How Black WWI Vets Fought Back Against Racist Mobs," *History*, last updated July 26, 2019, https://www.history.com/news/red -summer-1919-riots-chicago-dc-great-migration.

326. Higgins, "Red Summer of 1919: How Black WWI Vets Fought Back Against Racist Mobs."

327. David F. Krugler, "A Mob in Uniform: Soldiers and Civilians in Washington's Red Summer, 1919," *Washington History* 21 (2009): 48–77, https://www.jstor.org/stable /25704908.

328. Krugler, "A Mob in Uniform," 15.

329. Krugler, "A Mob in Uniform," 15.

330. Higgins, "Red Summer of 1919."

331. Cameron McWhirter, *Red Summer: The Summer of 1919 and the Awakening of Black America* (New York: St. Martin's Griffin, 2012).

332. Higgins, "Red Summer of 1919."

333. McWhirter, *Red Summer*.
334. Higgins, "Red Summer of 1919."

CHAPTER 30: WHAT WILL THE NEIGHBORS THINK?

335. Mary L. Dudziak, "Desegregation as a Cold War Imperative," *Stanford Law Review* 41, no. 1 (1988): 61–120, https://www.jstor.org/stable/1228836.
336. Dudziak, "Desegregation as a Cold War Imperative," 87.
337. Dudziak, "Desegregation as a Cold War Imperative," 90.
338. Dudziak, "Desegregation as a Cold War Imperative," 90.
339. Azza Salama Layton, "International Pressure and the U.S. Government's Response to Little Rock," *The Arkansas Historical Quarterly* 56, no. 3 (1997): 257–272, https://www.jstor.org/stable/40023174.
340. Dudziak, "Desegregation as a Cold War Imperative," 95, According to DuBois, the petition was not introduced in the United Nations for fear of harming the reputation of the U.S., however, the document received extensive coverage in the domestic and foreign press.
341. W.E.B. DuBois, "A Summary of This Petition (An Appeal to the World)," accessed April 18, 2022, https://credo.library.umass.edu/cgi-bin/pdf.cgi?id=scua:mums312-b229-i021.
342. Layton, "International Pressure and the U.S. Government's Response to Little Rock," 258, This followed the Justice Department's challenging of various school segregation cases, as well as cases involving housing discrimination.
343. Layton, "International Pressure and the U.S. Government's Response to Little Rock," 269.
344. John David Skrentny, "The Effect of the Cold War on African American Civil Rights: America and the World Audience, 1945-1968," *Theory and Society* 27, no. 2 (1998): 237–285, https://www.jstor.org/stable/657868.

CHAPTER 31: A NEGRO WITH A GUN

345. W.E.B. DuBois, "A Summary of This Petition (An Appeal to the World)."
346. Marcellus C. Barksdale, "Robert F. Williams and the Indigenous Civil Rights Movement in Monroe, North Carolina, 1961," *The Journal of Negro History* 69, no. 2 (1984): 73–89, www.jstor.org/stable/2717599.
347. Daren Salter, "Robert F. Williams (1925-1996)," *Blackpast.org*, December 9, 2007, https://www.blackpast.org/african-american-history/williams-robert-f-1925-1996.
348. Freedom Riders were individuals who participated in the Freedom Rides. "The Freedom Rides were first conceived in 1947 when CORE and the fellowship of Reconciliation, an interfaith fellowship group, organized an interracial bus ride across state lines to test a Supreme Court decision that declared segregation on interstate buses unconstitutional," Stanford University, "Freedom Rides."
349. Barksdale, "Robert F. Williams and the Indigenous Civil Rights Movement," 83–85.
350. Barksdale, "Robert F. Williams and the Indigenous Civil Rights Movement," 85.
351. Salter, "Robert F. Williams (1925-1996)."
352. Salter, "Robert F. Williams (1925-1996)."

CHAPTER 32: NEGROES WITH GUNS

353. Christopher B. Strain, "We Walked Like Men: The Deacons for Defense and Justice," *Louisiana History: The Journal of the Louisiana Historical Association* 38, no. 1 (1997): 43–62, https://www.jstor.org/stable/4233369.

354. Strain, "We Walked Like Men," 43–44.

355. Barksdale, "Robert F. Williams and the Indigenous Civil Rights Movement."

356. Stanford University, "White Citizens' Councils (WCC)," *The Martin Luther King, Jr. Research and Education Institute*, accessed March 25, 2022, https://kinginstitute .stanford.edu/encyclopedia/white-citizens-councils-wcc.

357. Strain, "We Walked Like Men," 43.

358. Strain, "We Walked Like Men," 50.

CHAPTER 33: THE KING'S SPEECH

359. Andrew Glass, "Reagan Establishes National Holiday for MLK, Nov. 2, 1983," *Politico*, last updated November 2, 2017, https://www.politico.com/story/2017/11/02 /reagan-establishes-national-holiday-for-mlk-nov-2-1983-244328.

360. Justoin Gomer and Christopher F. Petrella, "Reagan Used MLK Day to Undermine Racial Justice," BunkHistory.org, last updated January 15 2017, https://www .bunkhistory.org/resources/233.

361. Gomer and Petrella, "Reagan Used MLK Day to Undermine Racial Justice."

362. Martin Luther King Jr., "Beyond Vietnam—A Time to Break Silence," delivered April 4, 1967, New York, https://www.americanrhetoric.com/speeches /mlkatimetobreaksilence.html.

363. Martin Luther King Jr., "The Three Evils of Society," *National Conference on New Politics*, Delivered August 31, 1967, Chicago, https://www.nwesd.org/ed-talks/equity /the-three-evils-of-society-address-martin-luther-king-jr.

364. Jared A. Loggins and Andrew J. Douglas, *Prophet of Discontent: Martin Luther King Jr. and the Critique of Racial Capitalism* (Athens, GA: University of Georgia Press, 2021).

365. Martin Luther King Jr., *Where Do We Go From Here: Chaos or Community* (Boston, MA: Beacon Press, 2010).

366. King, "The Three Evils of Society."

367. Jeffrey M. Jones, "Americans Divided on Whether King's Dream Has Been Realized," last updated August 26, 2011, https://news.gallup.com/poll/149201 /americans-divided-whether-king-dream-realized.aspx.

368. Ariel Edwards-Levy, "In 1968, Nearly a Third of Americans Said MLK Brought His Assassination on Himself," *HuffPost*, last updated April 4, 2018, https://www.huffpost .com/entry/in-1968-nearly-a-third-of-americanssaid-mlk-brought-his-killing-on -himself_n_5ac51373e4b0aacd15b7d37b.

CHAPTER 34: FROM CIVIL RIGHTS TO HUMAN RIGHTS

369. Macolm X and George Breitman, *Malcolm X Speaks* (New York: Merit Publishers and Betty Shabazz, 1994).

370. Breitman, *Malcolm X Speaks*, 74–75.

371. Skrentny, "The Effect of the Cold War," 255.

372. Breitman, *Malcolm X Speaks*, 76.

373. Skrentny, "The Effect of the Cold War," 258.

374. Breitman, *Malcolm X Speaks*, 35.

375. United Nations Human Rights Council, The Promotion and Protection of the Human Rights and Undamental Freedoms of Africans and of People of African Descent Against Police Brutality and Other Violations of Human Rights, June 17, 2020.

CHAPTER 35: BLACK PANTHERS AROUND THE WORLD

376. JoNina M. Abron, "The Legacy of the Black Panther Party," *The Black Scholar* (2015): 33–37.

377. Jessica C. Harris, "Revolutionary Black Nationalism: The Black Panther Party," *The Journal of Negro History* 86, no. 3 (2001): 409–421, https://www.jstor.org/stable /1562458.

378. Harris, "Revolutionary Black Nationalism," 412.

379. Diane Pien, "Israeli Black Panther Party (1971–1977)."*BlackPast.org*, July 2, 2018, https://www.blackpast.org/global-african-history/israeli-black-panther-party-1971 -1977.

380. Pien, "Israeli Black Panther Party (1971–1977)."

381. Pien, "Israeli Black Panther Party (1971–1977)."

382. Pien, "Israeli Black Panther Party (1971–1977)."

383. Pien, "Israeli Black Panther Party (1971–1977)."

384. Pien, "Israeli Black Panther Party (1971–1977)."

385. Kathy Lothian, "Seizing the Time: Australian Aborigines and the Influence of the Black Panther Party, 1969–1972," *Journal of Black Studies* 35, no. 4 (2005): 179–200, https://www.jstor.org/stable/40027217.

386. Lothian, "Seizing the Time," 181.

387. "8 Things You Did Not Know About the Australian Black Panther Party," BlackHistoryStudies.com, accessed October 5, 2022, https://blackhistorystudies.com /resources/resources/australian-black-panther-party.

388. "8 Things You Did Not Know," BlackHistoryStudies.com.

389. Lothian, "Seizing the Time," 197.

CHAPTER 36: HOW THE KIDS GOT FREE BREAKFAST

390. Centers for Disease Control, "Eating Healthier at School," *CDC.gov*, last updated September 19, 2022, https://www.cdc.gov/healthyschools/features/eating_healthier .html.

391. Arielle Milkman, "The Radical Origins of Free Breakfast for Children," *Eater*, February 16, 2016, https://www.eater.com/2016/2/16/11002842/free-breakfast-schools -black-panthers.

392. United States Department of Agriculture, "The School Breakfast Program," USDA.gov, https://fns-prod.azureedge.us/sites/default/files/resourcefiles /SBPfactsheet.pdf.

393. Milkman, "The Radical Origins of Free Breakfast for Children."

394. Milkman, "The Radical Origins of Free Breakfast for Children."

395. Milkman, "The Radical Origins of Free Breakfast for Children."

396. Diane Pien, "Black Panther Party's Free Breakfast Program (1969-1980)," *BlackPast.org*, February 11, 2010, https://www.blackpast.org/african-american-history /black-panther-partys-free-breakfast-program-1969-1980.

397. Joshua Bloom and Waldo E. Martin Jr., *Black Against Empire: The History and Politics of the Black Panther Party* (Berkeley, CA: University of California Press, 2016).
398. Ruth Gebreyesus and Sana Javeri Kadri, "One of the Biggest, Baddest Things We Did: Black Panthers' Free Breakfasts, 50 Years On," *The Guardian*, last updated October 2018, https://www.theguardian.com/us-news/2019/oct/17/black-panther -party-oakland-free-breakfast-50th-anniversary."
399. Pien, "Black Panther Party's Free Breakfast Program (1969-1980)."
400. Potorti, Mary, "Feeding Revolution: The Black Panther Party and the Politics of Food," *Radical Teacher* 98 (2014): 43-50, https://radicalteacher.library.pitt.edu/ojs /index.php/radicalteacher/article/view/80.
401. Mary Potorti, "Feeding Revolution," 46.
402. Potorti, "Feeding Revolution," 46.
403. Pien, "Black Panther Party's Free Breakfast Program (1969-1980)."
404. Milkman, "The Radical Origins of Free Breakfast for Children."

CHAPTER 37: ROSA THE REVOLUTIONARY

405. Joe William Trotter Jr., "The Great Migration," *Organization of American Historians Magazine of History* 17, no. 1 (2002): 31-33, academic.oup.com/maghis /article-abstract/17/1/31/1060274.
406. Michael Schudson, "Telling Stories About Rosa Parks," *Contexts*, August 18, 2012, https://contexts.org/articles/telling-stories-about-rosa-parks.
407 Jeanne Theoharis and Say Burgin, "Pitting Rosa Parks against Claudette Colvin Distorts History," Washington Post, October 19, 2022, https://www.washingtonpost .com/made-by-history/2022/10/19/rosa-parks-documentary.
408. Schudson, "Telling Stories About Rosa Parks," 23.
409 Theoharis and Burgin, "Pitting Rosa Parks against Claudette Colvin."
410. Schudson, "Telling Stories About Rosa Parks," 23.
411. Aldon Morris, "Rosa Parks: Strategic Activist," *Contexts*, August 18, 2012, https:// contexts.org/articles/rosa-parks-strategic-activist.
412. Jeanne Theoharis, "'The Northern Promised Land that Wasn't:' Rosa Parks and the Black Freedom Struggle in Detroit," *Organization of American Historians Magazine of History* 26, no. 1 (2012): 23-27, https://academic.oup.com/maghis/article-abstract/26 /1/23/982201.
413. Theoharis, "The Northern Promised Land that Wasn't," 23.
414. Theoharis, "The Northern Promised Land that Wasn't," 24.
415. Theoharis, "The Northern Promised Land that Wasn't," 24.
416. Theoharis, "The Northern Promised Land that Wasn't," 25.
417. Theoharis, "The Northern Promised Land that Wasn't," 25.
418. Theoharis, "The Northern Promised Land that Wasn't," 27.
419. Theoharis, "The Northern Promised Land that Wasn't," 27.
420. Theoharis, "The Northern Promised Land that Wasn't," 27.

CHAPTER 38: MANDELA THE TERRORIST

421. Hermann Giliomee, "The Making of the Apartheid Plan, 1929-1948," *Journal of Southern African Studies* 29, no. 2 (2003): 374-392, https://www.jstor.org/stable /3557368.

422. The Martin Luther King Jr. Research & Education Institute, Apartheid, The Martin Luther King Jr. Research & Education Institute, May 31, 2022, https://kinginstitute.stanford.edu/encyclopedia/apartheid.

423. Katherine Schulz Richard, "Afrikaners," *Thought Co.*, last updated October 18, 2020, https://www.thoughtco.com/afrikaners-in-south-africa-1435512.

424. The Martin Luther King Jr. Research & Education Institute, "Apartheid."

425. Nelson Mandela Foundation, "Biography of Nelson Mandela," *NelsonMandela.org*, accessed May 3, 2022, https://www.nelsonmandela.org/content/page/biography.

426. Sabelo J. Ndlovu-Gatsheni, "From 'Terrorist' to Global Icon: A Critical Decolonial Ethical Tribute to Nelson Rolihlahla Mandela of South Africa," *Third World Quarterly* 35, no. 6 (2014): 905–921, https://www.tandfonline.com/doi/abs/10.1080/01436597.2014.907703.

427. Ndlovu-Gatsheni, "From 'Terrorist' to Global Icon," 908.

428. Ndlovu-Gatsheni, "From 'Terrorist' to Global Icon," 914.

429. Ndlovu-Gatsheni, "From 'Terrorist' to Global Icon," 908.

430. Caitlin Dewey, "Why Nelson Mandela was on a Terrorism Watch List in 2008," *The Washington Post*, last updated December 7, 2013, https://www.washingtonpost.com/news/the-fix/wp/2013/12/07/why-nelson-mandela-was-on-a-terrorism-watch-list-in-2008.

431. "Terrorist Group Profiles," accessed Ocotber 5, 2022, https://upload.wikimedia.org/wikipedia/commons/b/bb/Terrorist_Group_Profiles.pdf.

432. Richard Pyle, "Mandela Explains Support for PLO, Gadhafi, Castro with AM-Mandela," *Associated Press*, June 21, 1990, https://apnews.com/article/9412d3c54ecaff161e89f57f0225bde3.

433. Pyle, "Mandela Explains Support."

434. Dewey, "Why Nelson Mandela was on a Terrorism Watch List in 2008."

CHAPTER 39: WHY WE DAP

435. LaMont Hamilton, "Five on the Black Hand Side: Origins and Evolutions of the Dap," *Folk Life*, last updated September 22, 2014, https://folklife.si.edu/talkstory/2014/five-on-the-black-hand-sideorigins-and-evolutions-of-the-dap.

436. Rann Miller, "Does the Coronavirus Now Mean That I Can't Give 'Dap' Anymore?" *The Grio*, May 26, 2020, https://thegrio.com/2020/05/26/coronavirus-dap-black-handshake.

437. Hamilton, "Five on the Black Hand Side."

438. Hamilton, "Five on the Black Hand Side."

439. Miller, "Does the Coronavirus."

440. Robert Shuter, "The Dap in the Military," *Ethnic Studies In Black and White* 29, no. 1 (1979): 136–142, https:// academic.oup.com/joc/article-abstract/29/1/136/4371792.

441. A GI is a soldier. GI stands for "galvanized Iron."

442. Shuter, "The Dap in the Military," 136.

443. Hamilton, "Five on the Black Hand Side."

444. Miller, "Does the Coronavirus Now Mean That I Can't Give 'Dap' Anymore?"

ACKNOWLEDGMENTS

There are a number of individuals I must acknowledge for either inspiring and/or supporting the completion of this book.

I acknowledge my wife for her love and support during my time writing and researching. I appreciate her for her patience, for her parenting prowess, for being a great listener, and most importantly, for being an adviser through this whole process. She is truly brilliant. Her skill as a project manager made her truly indispensable during my period of scholarship and writing. Indeed, she is the love of my life.

I acknowledge my three children because this book was written for them. Parents desire to provide their children with an inheritance; I hope they'll consider this as part of the inheritance I leave them with. This book serves as their historical and culture inheritance. My prayers are that they not only learn from this book, but that they also pass it on to their children and grandchildren, as well as possibly add more stories of Black resistance to it. They are indeed my inspiration.

I acknowledge my father and mother, who invested time, talent, and treasure in my life that I would reside in this space as an educator. Without their love and commitment to me, I wouldn't be here.

I acknowledge Dr. Wayne Glasker for writing the foreword, for teaching me African American history, and affording me the high honor to serve as a guest lecturer in his courses. He was my first Black male teacher and his teaching opened the door to learning who I was and who I could be.

I acknowledge Dr. Katrina Hazzard-Donald for her teaching me about African American culture. She introduced me to the *quilombos* of Brazil. She also challenged me to think about Black culture that extends beyond U.S. borders, something unique in its Afrocentricity. Like Dr. Glasker, Dr. Hazzard-Donald is an intellectual heavyweight.

I acknowledge the continuum of governance spaces that have shaped the totality of my humanity. The barbershops and beauty salons, the Black Church, the family living rooms, the kitchen stoves, and the corner. Know that I love you.

I acknowledge Kierra Sondereker for extending the opportunity to put such a book together. This is a book that I've always wanted to write. I appreciate her for her support along the way, answering every question that came to mind and for believing in my ability to complete this project.

I acknowledge those of you who've purchased this book and have allowed me into both your intimate and communal spaces. I hope this book inspires you to learn more (Black) history and to inform your views of Black culture, Black history, and Black humanity.

Last, I acknowledge the significance of the number thirty-nine as it relates to this project. I was thirty-nine when writing this book. There are thirty-nine chapters or individual pieces in this book. Two individuals mentioned in this book were taken away from the Earth at age 39: Dr. Martin Luther King Jr. and el-Hajj Malik el-Shabazz. That is all to say I am humbled by the significance of this alignment.

I acknowledge those men and the host of other ancestors mentioned throughout this book. While teaching truth was a goal, it was my sincere ambition to humbly add to the honor and dignity of your stories.

My prayer is that I did just that.

ABOUT THE AUTHOR

Rann Miller is the anti-bias and DEI director for Camden's Promise Charter Schools in Camden, New Jersey. As an educator, Rann's work has included instructing students on conducting sound historical analysis and articulating one's voice, as well as supporting educators of all levels and locations via professional development workshops.

As a writer, Rann's work discussing the intersections of race, education, and politics is published on numerous platforms, including Edutopia, *Education Week*, the *Philadelphia Inquirer*, and the *Washington Post*. As a scholar, Rann's work on the topics of the disproportionate disciplining of Black students and Black educator motivations is peer-reviewed and published in various scholarly journals.

Rann is a graduate of Rutgers University with both his MS and MPA. He currently resides in Sicklerville, New Jersey, with his wife and three children.

Made in the USA
Coppell, TX
27 June 2023

18587667R00111